Walki

Step By Step Through Galatians

Daniel P. Fuller

Walking By the Spirit

Step By Step Through Galatians

Table of Contents

Foreword
Galatians 1:1–5 1
Galatians 1:6–2:10 2
Galatians 2:11–21 16
Galatians 3:1–18 29
Galatians 3:19–4:11 39
Galatians 4:12–5:1 55
Galatians 5:2–6; 5:13–6:18 64
Postscript 80
Final Words 83
Appendix: Paul's Application of Galatians 3:28 84
Bibliography 95

Foreword

Since the earliest days of the human race, we have been divided into two categories of people: those who worship the Creator and those who don't; those who humbly order their lives according to his design and those who proudly seek to achieve acclaim for what makes them distinctive. While this second category of people has displayed its disdain for God in every area of life, the arena of religious behavior has been a prominent one. Even the early Church struggled to walk on the right side of this divide, to follow Jesus in the obedience of faith. Because of his love for God's people of all nations, the Apostle Paul wrote a letter concerning this tendency to the non-Jewish congregations located in the Galatian region of Asia Minor (remnants of a Celtic population which migrated there approximately 300 years earlier), in order to persuade them to remain faithful to the Gospel message he proclaimed during his visit among them. While much of Paul's argument is easily accessible to the modern reader, some nuances of his train of thought are difficult to construe. Therefore we need secondary literary aides as we seek to understand his message, so we can apply it competently in today's dissonant and self-centered culture.

Daniel Fuller (Th. D., D. Theol., DD) has been "thinking God's thoughts after him" for many years. As the Professor of Hermeneutics at Fuller Theological Seminary, 1972–1993, he both taught and modeled the dedicated, honest work necessary to understanding what the biblical writers had to say. His most admirable trait, to those of us who were blessed to learn from him, is his consistent and humble submission to the text. In 1987, he committed to writing the years of study he invested in trying to understand and expound the details of Paul's epistle. In this work he took great pains to present reasons for each of his interpretive decisions, so that whoever used this work would understand why he holds the views he does, and would have a model for interacting with the text so they too could come to terms with the author. Even then, he was not entirely satisfied with his efforts; so he only published his work through the Fuller Seminary Bookstore. But now, nearly 30 years later, with some minor revisions, he has authorized release of this work.

Three notes regarding this version of the text: 1) Dr. Fuller uses the term "Judaizers" to identify Paul's opponents in Galatia. The term itself does not appear in the epistle itself, but it serves as a handy reference, which Dr. Fuller will fill with meaning as he works through the text. 2) The publishing software provides a limited number of fonts. So Greek words have been inserted using the "symbol" function of Microsoft Word. Therefore accent marks normally associated with these words in biblical texts are not available. 3) We have chosen to use the NET Bible® as the primary English text for this study. Small portions of text are attached to the various comments so the reader will be able to maintain close contact between the biblical words and the commentary. In some locations, Dr. Fuller has chosen to use his own translation to facilitate this connection; these texts are marked with this designation: [Fuller].

It has been a great pleasure for me to work through this material again as I have readied it for publication. I trust the Lord will grant you the joy of fellowship and a stronger faith as you use this tool to interact with the biblical text.

"For your progress and joy in the faith,"

Doug Knighton, Edmonds, WA, May 2016

Galatians 1:1–5

1:1–5 From Paul, an apostle (not from men, nor by human agency, but by Jesus Christ and God the Father who raised him from the dead) [2] and all the brothers with me, to the churches of Galatia. [3] Grace and peace to you from God the Father and our Lord Jesus Christ, [4] who gave himself for our sins to rescue us from this present evil age according to the will of our God and Father, [5] to whom be glory forever and ever! Amen.

Several features about 1:1–5 make the salutation of Galatians unique in contrast with the salutations of Paul's other epistles. Each feature provides evidence of Paul's being most angry with the Galatian readers: 1. He offers no thanksgiving for the Galatian Christians. 2. He does not call them "saints of God," but rather emphasizes his apostleship as a theological function Jesus' resurrection. 3. All the saints join with Paul in reprimanding the Galatians for their heresy, since it is so fundamentally wrong; it does not take church leaders like Timothy or Silas to point out its wrongness, but ordinary, grass-roots Christians ("all the brethren who are with me") join Paul in condemning it. 4. His benediction does not stand alone; he concludes it with a theological statement reaffirming the redemptive work accomplished by the Father and Son on the cross. Thus he sets the stage for the stinging rebuke which follows in 1:6ff.

Galatians 1:6–2:10

1:6–7 I am astonished that you are so quickly deserting the one who called you by the grace of Christ and are following a different gospel — ^{7} not that there really is another gospel, but there are some who are disturbing you and wanting to distort the gospel of Christ.

In most of Paul's letters he followed the custom of that time and gave thanks for his readers right after addressing them. So it is remarkable in Galatians that after opening the letter he goes on to speak instead about how much he is astounded at them. Paul marveled that the Galatians were ουτωσ ταξεωσ, "so quickly," turning aside from the gospel they had learned from him. He was also astonished that they would turn away from the *person*, God, who had called them in the grace of Christ, unto a mere *message*. ("I marvel that you would turn aside from *Him* who called you in the grace of Christ unto another gospel.") [Note: "grace" is construed in this commentary to indicate the exertions one makes, motivated by the joy in one's own life, to create a corresponding joy in another's life. So in this first use of the term, the "grace of Christ" should be understood as all that the supremely happy God has done through Jesus to bring people into a state in which they can rejoice in God as much as they are able.] The message preached by the Judaizers since Paul's last visit at Galatia was not just a small modification to what Paul had preached (as the Judaizers might have suggested). Their message was so different from Paul's message that it could not even be called a gospel, because its nature and the unloving motive of those preaching it would succeed only in troubling the Galatians (1:7; cf. 4:18; 6:13). So Paul's readers should realize that they are now on the verge of making a complete renunciation of their original faith (as the use of the verb μετατιθημι in 2 Maccabees 7:24, "turning from the ways of one's fathers" indicates). From the remaining words in verses 6 and 7 we understand why Paul marveled at what the Galatians were about to do. They were leaving the loving God to whom Paul had introduced them and were about to give allegiance to the Judaizers, whose message and motives would succeed only in abusing them.

1:8–9 But even if we (or an angel from heaven) should preach a gospel contrary to the one we preached to you, let him be condemned to hell! [9] As we have said before, and now I say again, if anyone is preaching to you a gospel contrary to what you received, let him be condemned to hell!

Paul was most astonished, however, that the Galatians were turning aside from the gospel to a message whose advocates, whoever they were, dwelt under the divine curse (ἀνάθεμα). To help the Galatians understand the divine condemnation under which the Judaizers stood, whose message they were about to embrace, he resorts to an *a fortiori* argument, "from the greater (in verse 8), to the lesser" (in verse 9). "Even if we apostles," says Paul (v. 8), "or an angel from heaven" were to preach a gospel different from what the Galatians had originally heard, they nevertheless would all be accursed by God for so doing. We note that v. 8 is set forth in hypothetical terms. No angels or apostles are preaching a different gospel, and so the main verb of the "if" clause is in the subjunctive mood and introduced by the conjunction ἐάν. But verse 9 speaks of those who are, in fact, preaching a different gospel. Here the main verb of the "if" clause is indicative and, accordingly, the conjunction introducing it is εἰ. So the truth of verse 9 receives great emphasis, because if angels and apostles would be under God's curse for ever preaching a different Gospel, then surely an ordinary person, signified by the τις of verse 9, will if possible be even more strongly accursed. So vv. 8 and 9 provide the climactic reason for Paul's astonishment in verse 6, where we would have expected a word of thanksgiving for the readers to have appeared.

Another way in which v. 9 is emphatic appears in the words by which Paul prefaces his second anathema: "As we said before, I also now say again ..." Both Schlier and Bruce think that the prior mention of the anathema about to be given in v. 9 is that just stated in v. 8. There is no evidence, Bruce argues, that on any previous occasion Paul had needed to warn the Galatians against the legalism of the Judaizers. To the contrary, 4:12 ff. and 5:7 ff. imply that up until now the Galatians had been running well, and had no difficulties submitting to Paul's apostleship. So the "as I said to you ..." introducing v. 9 refers to verse 8, because Paul wants the persuasive power it contains to carry over into verse 9 and help the Galatians realize that they are on the brink of discarding the one and only gospel. But what shall we make of "As *we* said before ..."? Only Paul had said verse 8, but by the use of the "we" he indicates that *all* the other apostles would join with him in anathematizing those presently preaching such falsehood in Galatia.

Several implications arise from Paul's placing himself within the band of other revelatory spokesmen by using "we" in verse 8 (emphatic use) and in the introduction to verse 9. For one thing Paul is saying that he is in accord with the other apostolic spokesmen, and not the purveyor of some strange teaching, as the Judaizers might well have been saying. (Note how Paul defends his apostleship in 1:1 and 11 f. and affirms it in 2:6–10, even though he had not been with Jesus while on earth [as had, for example, Peter and John].) Furthermore, since both Paul and the other apostles cited the Old Testament as the authority for their statements, these verses imply that he regarded himself and the other apostles as completing the Old Testament, and not setting it aside. This then has to mean that Paul regarded all that he, the other apostles, and the Old Testament taught as being a unity, for it is impossible to suppose that Paul thought that an anathema hung over any other apostle or over any Old Testament writer.

> **1:10** Am I now trying to gain the approval of people, or of God? Or am I trying to please people? If I were still trying to please people, I would not be a slave of Christ!

The obvious answer to the rhetorical questions, "Am I now trying to gain the approval of people or God, or do I seek to please people [instead of God]?" is that Paul is in the business of pleasing God and is persuading people to turn and live in a way that pleases God. Paul enforces this answer with the argument that were he still seeking to please men, he could not be Christ's servant. Introduced by the γαρ such questions with their obvious answers function to justify the imprecatory language Paul has used in the preceding two verses. Only one standing on God's side rather than man's would make such statements so sure to draw human anger and scoffing. Furthermore, verse 10 is useful for awakening the Galatians to agree with Paul that their inclination toward the Judaizers' teaching is most shocking and a just cause for his being astounded. For the Galatians to accept that teaching is tantamount to the absurdity of urging God to change his mind and seek to please sinful people by becoming the sort of God such people would prefer. Were they to agree with all that Paul has said in support of their present behavior's being very bizarre, then they would submit exclusively to Paul's teaching again. (But Bruce thinks it likely that the questions of verse 10 imply that one of the arguments the Judaizers were using against Paul was that he did accommodate to Jews when with them, and then to the Gentiles when with them [1 Corinthians 9:19 ff.; 10:33]. The problem with this interpretation, however, is that verse 10 says nothing that would be useful in countering such a charge and making Paul blameless again before his readers.)

> **1:11–12** Now I want you to know, brothers and sisters, that the gospel I preached is not of human origin. [12] For I did not receive it or learn it from any human source; instead I received it by a revelation of Jesus Christ.

1:11 The textual evidence for δε (disjunctive "and/now") as the connective introducing v. 11 is about equal to that for the γαρ (explanatory "for"). Schlier opts for the γαρ because he thinks that such radical language as Paul has just used can be justified best by one who bears the special title of an apostle, and so Paul proceeds to cite the evidence for his being appointed as Jesus' spokesman. Indeed, Schlier concedes that *anyone* who preaches Christ's gospel would be duty bound to make such statements against false teachers. But if all other preachers would have to speak just as Paul has spoken in 1:6–10, then Paul's defense of his apostleship in 1:11–2:10 serves some other purpose than simply that of justifying his imprecatory language in 1:8–9, and so δε would be the suitable conjunction. We have referred to the verses (1:1; 1:11–12; and 2:6–10) which provide evidence that the Judaizers at Galatia were denying that Paul was a revelatory spokesman in being an apostle. They may have disliked Paul because he told Gentiles they could inherit Abraham's blessing simply by faith and with no need to be circumcised or submit to a kosher diet. Then they could well have argued that his teaching needed correction because it clashed with the teaching of the Old Testament and that of the other apostles. So in order to show that he is an apostle (a revelatory spokesman), he reviews the historical evidence supporting his claim to be an apostle. His gospel is not κατα ανθροπον (according to a human being; v. 11), which means that his gospel is a divine message rather than a human one. The reason he uses γνωριζω (to make known publicly) is not that he is telling the Galatians and the Judaizers his conversion story for the first time, as the "you have heard" of v. 13 makes clear. Rather the use of this word indicates that he reverts to his long-standing policy of telling everyone about his remarkable turn from zeal for Pharisaism to zeal for promoting a Gentile mission, which, unlike the Pharisees' missionary endeavors (cf. Matthew 23:15), does not impose Jewish distinctives on would-be converts.

1:12 The ουδε (neither) before the emphatic εγω (I) is Paul's tacit admission that the circumstances by which he became an apostle were quite unlike those of the other apostles, who had been with Jesus some time before their commissioning. "For neither did I receive the Gospel nor was I taught it from men, but rather through a revelation from Jesus Christ." To be sure, Paul spoke of receiving from men (παραλαμβον — same as the word for "received" in this verse) the words Christ used at the last supper (1 Corinthians 11:23) and the saving events of the resurrection tradition (1 Corinthians 15:3). But there was a special part of the gospel that Jesus revealed only to Paul, and that was a theological understanding of how the gospel was to go to the "nations," the multitude of non-Jewish ethnic entities, without requiring such to take on Jewish cultural distinctives (1:15 ff.; cf. Ephesians 3:1–13). Since it was just this particular contribution of Paul's which the Judaizers wanted to deny, Paul proceeds to argue that this contribution was apostolic, that it came directly from Jesus, by revelation, and not at all from his own imagination or from some other purportedly Christian teacher.

1:13–18 For you have heard of my former way of life in Judaism, how I was savagely persecuting the church of God and trying to destroy it. [14] I was advancing in Judaism beyond many of my contemporaries in my nation, and was extremely zealous for the traditions of my ancestors. [15] But when the one who set me apart from birth and called me by his grace was pleased [16] to reveal his Son in me so that I could preach him among the Gentiles, I did not go to ask advice from any human being, [17] nor did I go up to Jerusalem to see those who were apostles before me, but right away I departed to Arabia, and then returned to Damascus. [18] Then after three years I went up to Jerusalem to visit Cephas and get information from him, and I stayed with him fifteen days.

1:13–14 Far from simply making the affirmation of v. 12, he proceeds to argue for it (hence the γαρ introducing v. 13). "You have heard ..." Paul begins the argument for his apostleship on common knowledge that is already in place. "You have heard" starts his argument for his apostleship with what is more a matter of general knowledge than would be implied by "I told you" (which was probably the way the Galatians first learned of Paul's life in Judaism [ιουδαισμω]). This is not the word for what the Old Testament teaches, but for what is distinctive about the Jewish religion (cf. the verbal use in 2:14). "Judaism" was what once characterized his behavior, his conduct (ανα-στροπην). The rest of v. 13 and 14 then relates three noteworthy aspects of this behavior. These are set forth by verbs in the imperfect tense to show that these were a continuing part of his behavior during that period and stemmed from his deepest convictions.

1. He was persecuting the church of God beyond measure. The imperfect tense of "persecuted," the "beyond measure," and

2. the sacking, or laying waste the church (επορθουν) — these indicate how Judaism led Paul to be completely given over to persecuting the church. This serves his argument for 1:12 by indicating that his heart was so completely behind his persecuting zeal that it was psychologically impossible for him to have been influenced toward Christianity by any of the Christians he persecuted or by anything he had heard about Christianity's teachings. Hence, the great change that occurred in his behavior, not only in becoming a Christian, but more particularly in carrying out the Gentile mission, had to come from some source outside of Paul and his environment. Further support for this conclusion comes from the third imperfect:

3. "I was advancing in Judaism ..." Paul was not drifting toward Christianity; rather, he was repelled by it and became more zealous for the distinctives of Judaism, because Christians were implying that these distinctives had no value in improving one's

standing with God. Christian Jews had been teaching Jews that in order to have the forgiveness of sins, they needed to repent and be baptized in the name of Jesus.). Of all the young, up-and-coming Pharisees, Paul was the most zealous for the Pharisaic traditions, and therefore the one who would take most offense at what the church was preaching. F. F. Bruce says, "The 'traditions' would be more particularly those enshrined in the oral law ... or *halakhah* handed down in Pharisaic schools" (p. 91). Verse 14 then ends on the note with which v. 13 began, viz., that of "Judaism" and "tradition of the fathers." This emphasizes that all the behavior in between arose from allegiance to Judaism. Therefore a supernatural cause is required for explaining why Paul henceforth acted in a way so opposite from this Judaism in which he had been so engrossed.

1:15–18 Verses 15–16a are essentially a temporal clause; verses 16b–17 are the main clause. What happened in the temporal clause, especially, "When God ... was pleased to reveal his Son to me, in order that I might preach him among the Gentiles," caused Paul to stay away from Jerusalem for three years. This is emphasized by the strange wording at the beginning of the main clause: " ... *immediately* I did not confer with flesh and blood, nor did I go up to Jerusalem to those who were apostles before me." That Paul should "immediately" *not* do these things is perhaps the strongest way to convey the idea that the happening of the temporal clause left Paul with absolutely no choice but to stay away from the other apostles, who were residing at Jerusalem, in order that he might look to God rather than the other apostles while he revised his thinking away from Pharisaism and his persecution of Jesus' church, to a thinking which turned on Jesus' being Lord and Savior for all the peoples of earth. This explains all the verbs of the main clause, each of which contributes to Paul's need to stay away from Jerusalem for the "three years" (v. 18) necessary for him to fully develop his thinking, and only then visit Peter and James for two weeks just to get acquainted (ἱστορησαι). Sometime during this period Paul could well have received the traditional teaching about the Christian religion alluded to in 1 Corinthians 1:23 and 15:3 ff. So the two-week, get-acquainted visit to Jerusalem after these three years was hardly sufficient for Paul to have received his teaching "from men" (cf. 1:12). That had been worked out during the two or

8

three years he had studiously avoided going back to Jerusalem. Accounting for such behavior in one who had previously made his residence in Jerusalem where he had been so zealously defending the traditions of Judaism is done most easily by accepting Paul's explanation that God revealed his Son — and all that this meant — to Paul, particularly in view of the Gentile mission that Paul was to carry out. But while Paul's having become an apostle required him to remain aloof from the other apostles for a considerable time, it also required that he make evident his concurrence with them, for otherwise there would be evidence for the Judaizers' charge that Paul was a spurious Christian teacher, and not in harmony with the leading apostles at Jerusalem. In this way, then, vv. 15–18 function to support the thesis of 1:12, that Paul was an apostle by virtue of an immediate revelation from Jesus Christ himself.

1:19–24 But I saw none of the other apostles except James the Lord's brother. [20] I assure you that, before God, I am not lying about what I am writing to you! [21] Afterward I went to the regions of Syria and Cilicia. [22] But I was personally unknown to the churches of Judea that are in Christ. [23] They were only hearing, "The one who once persecuted us is now proclaiming the good news of the faith he once tried to destroy." [24] So they glorified God because of me.

That Paul saw only Peter and James during a fortnight visit (v. 19) emphasizes that he was not an understudy of these apostles and of some teachers at Jerusalem, but was simply showing his oneness with them by paying a visit to two of them. The fitting thing to do by one who had relatively recently been appointed by Jesus to be his spokesman was to pay a visit to the two apostles who had been the leaders of the Church at Jerusalem from its beginning. Furthermore, Paul's taking an oath in support of the matters just related (v. 20) strengthens the credibility of what he has said: he has no fear of bringing terrible divine judgment down on him for posing as an apostle, because he knows he has not been lying, vv. 21–24. That Paul had no need for being an understudy to the other apostles or teachers at Jerusalem is further emphasized by his decision to go to Syria and Cilicia (v. 21), a region completely removed from Jerusalem. According to vv. 22 f., his conduct was such that he continued to remain unknown (periphrastic participle) by face to the Christian churches of Judea. These churches were only hearing (for Paul was now far away from Jerusalem) that he who once was persecuting them is now preaching the faith he once was destroying. This gives further evidence that there was no period in the apostle Paul's early days for him to have been instructed by the apostles who were congregated in Judea. According to v. 24, the only explanation the Judean church could give for this remarkable turnabout in Paul was that God had worked, and thus they were praising God for making him an apostle. The implication is that the Galatians should come to the same conclusion and, glorifying God for Paul, reject the Judaizers' claim that he was a renegade Christian teacher.

2:1–10 Paul's purpose in this paragraph is to adduce more historical evidence that he is Jesus' apostle. As in 1:18–24, so here in 2:1–10, he does things that show his independence from other apostles, but also his desire to demonstrate his agreement with them. Since he and they were acting on orders from Jesus Christ who had ordained them to be apostles, then a rift between them must be avoided, to avoid a fatal injury to the Church. In vv. 1–5 Paul sets forth Jerusalem and its leaders as *tacitly* approving of his Gentile mission by acknowledging against the strongest opposition that the uncircumcised Gentile Christian, Titus, wore the proper sign of the covenant in his having been baptized. Vv. 6–10 set forth how the chief apostles at Jerusalem *explicitly* approved of Paul's Gentile mission without seeking to modify his leading of it in any way.

> **2:1** Then after fourteen years I went up to Jerusalem again with Barnabas, taking Titus along too.

"After fourteen years again I went up to Jerusalem" — As Paul went about his peculiar apostolic work of advancing the Gentile mission, there was no need during this considerable period of time to have dealings with the Jerusalem apostles. Thus Paul was acting independently, as one would expect of an apostle with a special mission from the Lord. But his Gentile mission increasingly created a tension with the Jerusalem church, because so many Gentiles were becoming Christians with nothing being said about their need to be circumcised. So when this tension reached a crisis point, Paul came to Jerusalem with Barnabas, who had close ties with the Jerusalem church (Acts 4:36; 9:27; 11:22), and, as a supervisor of the Jewish and Gentile church at Antioch, had played a key role in getting Paul's Gentile mission started. Paul also brought the uncircumcised Gentile convert, Titus, so that the Jerusalem church, faced by him, would have to come to an unambiguous decision as to whether or not Gentile believers needed to be circumcised.

> **2:2** I went there because of a revelation and presented to them the gospel that I preach among the Gentiles. But I did so only in a private meeting with the influential people, to make sure that I was not running—or had not run—in vain.

Paul went up to Jerusalem "by revelation." Paul's reason for going there was not because as a subordinate of the Jerusalem apostles he was summoned to give account of himself. Instead he went there as one who took his orders from Jesus Christ. At Jerusalem Paul laid before (αναθεμεν) the whole church, but more particularly its leaders, the very gospel which he is preaching (present tense) among the Gentiles. He wanted to make evident a genuine harmony with the Jerusalem apostles; in order for this to happen, he could not try to hide any aspects of his Gentile mission. So Paul dealt with the church's acknowledged leaders and not merely with some influential people representing only one strand of the Jerusalem church. There were groups of people representing different convictions in that church. There were even "false brethren" who had enough eminence to be at the meeting where the decision about Titus was made (v. 4). But the decision made by "those of repute" (James, Peter, and John — v. 9) prevailed over the will of this strand of influential people. In that the decision about Titus went against the desire of these people, it also went against the Judaizers at Galatia. Thus Paul showed his readers the historical evidence that the Judaizers, rather than he, were at odds with the leaders at Jerusalem — "lest perhaps I am running or had run in vain." Paul had no doubts in his own mind that his gospel was true, but he knew that unless the primary authorities at Jerusalem agreed with his gospel, then the argument against his Gentile mission, such as the Judaizers were now making at Galatia, would prevail and turn Gentile converts away from him. As Bruce puts it, "[Paul's] commission was not derived from Jerusalem, but it could not be executed effectively except in fellowship with Jerusalem" (p. 111).

> **2:3–5** Yet not even Titus, who was with me, was compelled to be circumcised, although he was a Greek. [4] Now this matter arose because of the false brothers with false pretenses who slipped in unnoticed to spy on our freedom that we have in Christ Jesus, to make us slaves. [5] But we did not surrender to them even for a moment, in order that the truth of the gospel would remain with you.

2:3 "Compelled" implies that the strongest possible argument was made for having Titus circumcised. The words "not even Titus" indicate that this strongest argument which Paul's opponent could mount was not able to win over the authorities in the Jerusalem church. For the readers at Galatia this would mean that Paul's Gentile mission had been opposed by every possible argument set forth before the authorities in Jerusalem, and yet these authorities had sided with Paul.

2:4 The attempt to have Titus circumcised was really made "on account of the false brethren brought in alongside, who came in alongside to spy out this freedom of ours which we are having in Christ, in order that they might enslave us." That these people entered this all-important meeting between "those of repute," on the one hand, and Paul and Titus, on the other, indicates the strong motivation of Paul's opponents to change the Gentile mission radically. In this adversarial contest, they put Paul's teaching to the strongest test. Hence the victory he gained becomes all the more significant. The designations of Paul's opponents as "false brothers," "spies," "not belonging to the main stream" (since they came in alongside), and "slave-makers," forcefully drives home the inferences to be drawn from the adverse decision rendered against them. These designations extend by implication to the Judaizers at Galatia. Then too, Paul's reference to *our* freedom which *we* are enjoying puts him and his readers at Galatia together in Christ, where they are enjoying a glorious freedom, while the Judaizers are placed outside as enslavers and looking in at possible victims. In evoking such a picture in his readers' minds, Paul was imparting a powerful persuasive for regaining his converts' loyalty.

2:5 "Yield in submission" is a pleonasm develop
the readers the horrible slavery to which the rea
thinking of surrendering. "Even for a moment" co.
seriously the Galatians are considering the decision to
to the Judaizers. "That the truth of the gospel might rema   ou."
Had the decision at Jerusalem gone against Paul, then c. .mcision
would have been mandatory for Gentiles to become Christians. This
requirement would have brought the Gentile mission to a halt, and the
gospel would not even have come as far as Galatia. Indeed Paul
would have been more accurate to speak of his and Barnabas' acting
"that the truth of the Gospel might *come* to you," than "*remain* with
you." But Paul wanted his readers now to make the same decision he
and Barnabas had made in not yielding to the false brethren. In order
to get them into this mode of thinking, he uses the word "remain,"
since everything (the truth!) now depends on their not yielding to the
Judaizers' arguments.

> **2:6–10** But from those who were influential (whatever they
> were makes no difference to me; God shows no favoritism be-
> tween people)--those influential leaders added nothing to my
> message. [7] On the contrary, when they saw that I was entrust-
> ed with the gospel to the uncircumcised just as Peter was to
> the circumcised [8] (for he who empowered Peter for his
> apostleship to the circumcised also empowered me for my
> apostleship to the Gentiles) [9] and when James, Cephas [Peter],
> and John, who had a reputation as pillars, recognized the grace
> that had been given to me, they gave to Barnabas and me the
> right hand of fellowship, agreeing that we would go to the
> Gentiles and they to the circumcised. [10] They requested only
> that we remember the poor, the very thing I also was eager to
> do.

2:6 "But from those seeming to be something ..." In the interests of
harmony Paul acknowledges that the influential Jerusalem apostles do
have the credentials of authority. But this expression also shows
Paul's independence from these leaders, for there is a derogatory
sound in denoting them as "seeming to be something." The repute of
Peter and John derived from their having been with Jesus during his
earthly ministry. James, as Jesus' brother (1:19), was at the top of the

even above Peter (2:9). He had been an unbeliever during Jesus' lifetime (Mark 3:21; 31–35; cf. John 7:3–5), but Jesus made him an apostle by appearing to him after Easter (1 Corinthians 15:7). With justification, therefore, Paul argues that "what they once were [Peter and John in being Jesus' disciples, and James in being Jesus' brother] makes no difference to me; God shows no partiality." So Paul regards himself to be a peer with the Jerusalem apostles. What was essential for them to be apostles was that they, like Paul, were commissioned to preach by the risen Jesus (cf. 1 Corinthians 9:1 f.). Paul had started to say at the beginning of v. 6, "But from those of repute at Jerusalem [I received no instructions about how to carry on my Gentile mission]. But before the end of v. 6 he changed the structure of the sentence from that which would have asserted that he had initiated an action expressing agreement between him and the Jerusalem apostles, to that in which they initiate such an action. (This change may also show that he desired, from his side, to work in harmony with them, but then he remembers how important it is for him to act as fully an apostle in his own right.) So the newly structured sentence reads, "For those of re-pute added nothing to me ... but they gave me and Barnabas the right hand of fellowship (vv. 6c, 9)." The "for" in the newly structured sen-tence introduces it as an argument for why he remained unyielding to the false brethren (v. 5). "*Added nothing.*" In 1:16 Paul used this verb in the middle voice to say that "immediately I did not confer with flesh and blood," to receive help in developing his apostolicity. Used in the active voice in 2:6, it sounds the same note of apostolic inde-pendence: "The apostles added nothing to me." So Paul again empha-sizes both his good standing with the other apostles as well as his in-clination (essential for an apostle) to act independently as Jesus' spokesman. This statement thus helps support Paul's thesis made back at 1:12, that he is an apostle "not of men neither through men, but through a revelation from Jesus Christ."

2:7–9 Verses 7 and 8 set forth the causes explaining the action in the main clause of v. 9, where the Jerusalem apostles gave Paul the right hand of fellowship and acknowledged that he and Barnabas had a God-given ministry to the Gentiles.

2:7 The Jerusalem apostles saw that Paul "had been entrusted with the gospel for the Gentiles, just as Peter had been entrusted with the gospel for the circumcision." This tells the Galatians that James, Peter, and John acknowledged Paul's authority.

2:8 Their reason for doing so was that they realized that "[God] who had energized Peter for an apostleship for the circumcision had also energized me [Paul] for [an apostleship] unto the Gentiles." Paul here was implying that he, like Peter, has a specific apostleship. But he allows this affirmation to be made implicitly in supplying the ellipsis in the statement about himself that is parallel with the statement about Peter. Betz thinks that the omission of the word "apostle" for Paul means that the Jerusalem apostles never regarded Paul as an apostle. But if this were the reason for the omission, then Paul would have been conceding the Judaizers' claim that he was not an apostle. It is much easier to think (with Schlier) that Paul is affirming, by implication, his own apostleship. With the "just as" of verse 7, the "also" of verse 8, and "the right hand of fellowship" (v. 9), Paul emphasizes his equality with Peter and the other Jerusalem apostles. Then too, for Paul not to supply the ellipsis in the parallel clause of verse 8 means that Paul avoided the awkwardness of vaunting his apostleship at the expense of mechanically supplying implicit words in an ellipsis.

2:9 Thus with the knowledge that Paul had a ministry, by grace, that was equivalent to Peter's, then "James, Peter, and John, those reputed to be pillars [and thus have the final authority at Jerusalem], gave to me and Barnabas the right hand of fellowship."

2:10 Paul concludes this section with a reference to the Jerusalem leaders' openness for monetary help from the Gentile churches. But to this Paul responds that he has been most eager to cement the bond between the Jewish and Gentile Christians by having the latter send money to Jerusalem. See 1 Corinthians 16:1–4, which mentions that the Galatians have taken part in the collection being gathered for the Jerusalem saints.

Galatians 2:11–21

F. F. Bruce observes that this paragraph is not introduced by επειτα (then, next), as 1:18–24 and 2:1–10 were, to be a follow up on Paul's conversion experience. Then too, in this paragraph Paul is saying things which could help the Judaizers make good their claim that he was at odds with the chief apostles. So we argue that Paul has now moved on from establishing that he is a bona fide apostle (1:11–2:10) to where he now puts 1:8 into practice and points up Peter's own self-condemnation for having acted inconsistently with the truth of the gospel. Not just apostles, but all servants of Christ, who seek to please God rather than men (cf. 1:10), will stand for God against an apostle or even an angel who advocates, either by word or practice, a message different from that proclaimed in concert by the revelatory spokesmen (cf. 1:8). So in this passage Paul begins his theological argument for the validity of this apostolic message by relating how he once had to rebuke Peter publicly before the church at Antioch. Another evidence that the purpose of 2:11–14 is theological, and is no longer a defense of Paul's apostolicity, comes from how 2:15–21 flows naturally from the way Paul had confronted Peter at Antioch, into a theological argument defending the stand that both Peter and Paul had once taken, that one could be justified only by faith in Christ. This is set forth by the "we" pronouns in vv. 15–17, as though Paul were still recounting the argument against Peter before the Antiochean church. But in vv. 18–21 he shifts to the "I", because having now shown that Peter, despite his misstep at Antioch, had really believed all along as Paul, he is now able to stand up against the Judaizers at Galatia — now with Peter right alongside him — and declare that if righteousness comes in any other way than simply through faith in Christ, then Jesus' death on the cross was in vain.

> **2:11–14** But when Cephas [Peter] came to Antioch, I opposed him to his face, because he had clearly done wrong. [12] Until certain people came from James, he had been eating with the Gentiles. But when they arrived, he stopped doing this and separated himself because he was afraid of those who were pro-circumcision. [13] And the rest of the Jews also joined with him in this hypocrisy, so that even Barnabas was led astray with them by their hypocrisy. [14] But when I saw that they were

not behaving consistently with the truth of the gospel, I said to Cephas in front of them all, "If you, although you are a Jew, live like a Gentile and not like a Jew, how can you try to force the Gentiles to live like Jews?"

"But when Peter came to Antioch I withstood him to his face, because he stood condemned." The periphrastic use of the participle (perfect passive, εν καταγνωσμενος) with a tense (imperfect) of the verb "to be" imparts the meaning that Peter stood self-condemned (lit. "was having been condemned"). Verse 11 gives the upshot of the whole incident. Vv. 12–14 relate what led up to this self-condemnation.

2:12 "Before the coming of certain people from James, Peter had been carrying on table fellowship (συνησθιεν) with the Gentile Christians." The imperfect tense of this verb indicates that Peter's eating a non-kosher diet with the Gentile Christians had been his regular practice for some time. "But when those from James came, he gradually withdrew [imperfect] and separated [imperfect] himself [from table fellowship with Gentiles], because he feared those of the circumcision." Apparently there was a group in the Jerusalem church who felt so strongly about adherence to Jewish customs (cf. Acts 21:21) that they prevailed upon James to send a team to Antioch to check out reports that Jewish members of that church were giving up these customs. Peter seemed to fear that if this group at Jerusalem was not pleased with the report that came back, they might create a schism in the Jerusalem church that would insist, contrary to the decision of the pillars (2:9), on breaking off all contact between Jewish believers and uncircumcised Gentile Christians. Peter, no less than Paul, wanted to avoid such a cleavage, and so he withdrew from table fellowship with Gentile Christians. And he withdrew gradually, in the hope that his absence might escape the Gentile believers' notice. The best explanation for this gradual withdrawal is that he feared that the Gentile believers would conclude from his reversion to a kosher diet, that they also must learn to eat as Jews in order to be genuine Christians.

But Peter's plan went awry. According to v. 13, the rest of the Jewish believers, and even Barnabas, followed Peter's example and left off table fellowship with the Gentiles, and as Paul puts it in v. 15, this indeed compelled the Gentiles to believe they had to live like Jews, if they wanted to go on being Christians.

2:13 Two times in this verse Paul characterizes the actions of Peter and the Jewish believers at Antioch as hypocrisy, because such actions transmitted a message that was contrary to their deepest convictions. By suddenly eating kosher food when the emissaries from James arrived, they were falsely implying to these visitors that they had been adhering, all along, to a kosher diet, when they had always been eating (cf. the imperfect tense of "they were eating" — v. 12) Gentile food while fellowshipping with the believers at Antioch. Furthermore, in switching over suddenly to a kosher diet, Peter and Barnabas, as the most prominent Jerusalem Christians, were now saying to the Gentile Christians at Antioch that kosher eating had been an essential part of being a Christian all along, but that they had been false teachers by failing to go on eating this way. As a result the Gentiles at Antioch now concluded that they must learn to eat kosher food in order to be true Christians. But Peter Richardson, "Pauline Inconsistency: 1 Corinthians 9:19–23 and Galatians 2:11–14" (*New Testament Studies*, 26,3[1979/80]), says, "Peter's action should not be viewed as hypocrisy but as an attempt (obviously unacceptable to Paul) to engage in a similar kind of accommodation to that which Paul espouses. They differ only in their views of the circumstances in which one should adopt such an ethic" (p. 348). But then Richardson goes on to say, "Antioch is the foremost church in a gentile area; here, of all places, it would be incorrect to give in to Jewish predispositions or even to Jewish Christian wishes if that were going to compromise the privileges won for Gentile Christians and just alluded to by Paul in Galatians 2:6 ff." (p. 352). So even Richardson admits that Peter was wrong, after all, in giving in to Jewish "predispositions and prejudices" at the expense of the benefits that Paul had won for Gentile Christians in Galatians 2:6. *"Even Barnabas"* — This indicates Peter's great influence and the power of his reversion to a kosher diet radically to change the life style of the many ordinary Jewish believers at Antioch, so that *even* Barnabas, the full-time pastor there, reverted to Jewish behavior, despite the many Gentile believers in his flock at Antioch.

18

2:14 Having established in verses 12 and 13 (1) the sheer hypocrisy of what Peter did, and yet (2) the prevailing power of his influence to get all the Jews in the Antiochean church to submit to this hypocrisy, Paul was now able in v. 14 to show up in one "if-then" sequence how wrongly Peter had taught the church at Antioch through his desire not to split the church at Jerusalem, ει, "if," has the virtual power of "since," in that everyone agreed that although Peter was born and bred as a Jew (ὑπαρχων Ιουδαιος), yet he was living (ζης — pr. tense) not as a Jew but as a Gentile. The reason Peter had been, until recently, acting so contrary to his cultural roots was that he joined Barnabas and Paul in accommodating outward toward the Gentiles and away from Judaism, in order that the Gentiles might understand that salvation had nothing to do with adhering to Jewish cultural distinctives. It depended rather upon one's having his or her faith (or hope) banked on the promises of God summed up in Christ. But now Peter had reverted to a Jewish life style while continuing to reside at Antioch. His unsurpassed influence as an apostle of Jesus compelled the Jewish believers in the church at Antioch, and even Barnabas, to revert to a Jewish life style. Consequently, the Gentile believers felt *compelled* to take on a Jewish life style in order to remain in fellowship with their Jewish leaders from Jerusalem, the origin of Christianity. Paul's question, "How can you compel the Gentiles to become Jewish?" conveys the idea of the impossibility of doing this. It was *impossible* to think that thousands of ethnic entities (yet to be reached), extending out to the ends of the earth would, each be willing to set aside its own cultural heritage and submit to Jewish customs climaxing in the difficulty of being circumcised. (Betz points to 5:3 as being a parallel to 2:14, "If you receive circumcision, you are obligated to keep all the law [i.e., all the Jewish cultural distinctives].") What Peter had done was also *impossible* because it made circumcision and other Jewish distinctives "something," when, in fact, they were "nothing," and all that counted was a confidence directed away from one's own distinctives and abilities, toward the promises of God in Christ (cf. 5:6; 6:15). Paul elaborates on the impossibility of what Peter had done in 2:15 ff..

2:15–21 We are Jews by birth and not 'Gentile sinners,' [16] yet we know that no one is justified by the works of the law but by the faithfulness of Jesus Christ. And we have come to believe in

Christ Jesus, so that we may be justified by the faithfulness of Christ and not by the works of the law, because by the works of the law no one will be justified. [17] But if while seeking to be justified in Christ we ourselves have also been found to be sinners, is Christ then one who encourages sin? Absolutely not! [18] But if I build up again those things I once destroyed, I demonstrate that I am one who breaks God's law. [19] For through the law I died to the law so that I may live to God. [20] I have been crucified with Christ, and it is no longer I who live, but Christ lives in me. So the life I now live in the body, I live because of the faithfulness of the Son of God, who loved me and gave himself for me. [21] I do not set aside God's grace, because if righteousness could come through the law, then Christ died for nothing!

Note: that "we" is used emphatically, and that it appears twice in this sentence comprising verses 15 and 16. The "we" includes Paul and Peter as Jews "by nature" (φυσει).

2:15 commences with the sense, "*Although* we are Jews by nature and not sinners of the Gentiles ... ," because what Paul and Peter had done, according to the main clause of v. 16 — "even we have believed in Jesus Christ," was done *despite* this Jewishness. According to the Judaism out of which Paul and Peter came they were very different from "sinners of the Gentiles." Betz has cited 2 Maccabees 6:12–17 as providing a glimpse of how Jews regarded Gentiles to be sinners in a different sense from the way Jews were. "[In this passage] the sins of the Gentiles are punished with a goal of destruction (προς αλεθρον), while Jewish sinners are merely disciplined (προς παιδεαιν)." (Betz, p. 115, n. 27.) So Jews, on the basis of their Jewishness, enjoyed a considerable confidence of being saved despite their sins, but the Gentiles could look forward only to God's destroying them for their sins.

2:16 commences with the sense, "but *because* we knew that a person is not justified by works of the law but only by the faithfulness of Christ," for it leads to the conclusion of the main clause, namely, *therefore* "[Peter and Paul] have believed in Jesus Christ." The causal clause on which this conclusion is based is taken from Psalm 143 (LXX 142):2, "Enter not into judgment with your servant, for in your sight no man living is just," for Paul restates it at the end of v. 16 by quoting Psalm 143:2 explicitly. The nub of the argument in this citation is that *since* every one has sinned and is thus guilty before God, *therefore* forgiveness comes not through "works of law" but only through the faithfulness of Christ. C. E. B. Cranfield, "St. Paul and the Law," *SJT* 17(1964), p. 55, and C. F. D. Moule, "Obligation in the Ethic of Paul," *Knox FS*, p. 392, have argued that as Paul had no ready word or phrase for "legalism," he sometimes used the word "law," or a phrase having "law" in it, such as "works of law," to signify legalism. Context alone indicates whether νομος was used in the sense of what the "revelatory law" of Moses intended to say, or in a legalistic sense to represent how Judaism has perverted the intended meaning of the revelatory law. F. F. Bruce agrees to the extent of saying that "legalism" is the meaning now conveyed by Paul's use of the word "law" (pp. 137 f.), and that "works of law," used three times in v. 16, represents the legalistic idea (to use Barrett's phrase) "of an upward striving of human religion and morality ..." Bruce believes that this term represented Paul's pre-Christian record in which "as to righteousness in the law" he was "blameless" (Philippians 3:6). "But [Paul] learned that *even* this record did not justify him before God" (p. 138, italics added). According to Bruce, the words "even this record" imply that Paul's effort during his pre-Christian days was good so far as it went, because the revelatory law itself taught legalism. It is not difficult to understand how Bruce can speak of a legalistic idea of the law that is not a perversion of the *revelatory* law's meaning. After all is said and done, the meaning Bruce gives to the 3-fold "works of law" in v. 16 is simply to make the "legalism" of trying to do what the law commands a part of what the revelatory law commands and not a perversion of that law. Far from there being any difference between legalism and the revelatory law, he sees the revelatory law as legalizing legalism.

There are, however, several considerations with respect to the flow of thought from 2:11–16 which indicate that such a meaning as Bruce advocates for "works of law" in 2:16 would be irrelevant. One consideration is that verse 16 comes right after the paragraph recounting Paul's clash with Peter at Antioch on the matter of Jewish dietary regulations (2:11-14). As Paul relates it, his clash with Peter was not over the question of whether or not a person should try to keep the law perfectly in order to be saved, but only over whether or not Gentile believers needed to take on such Jewish cultural distinctives as a kosher diet in order to benefit fully from the salvation made possible by Christ. By the use of the "we" in verses 15 and 16, Paul gives the reader to understand that in these verses he is still recounting how he had spoken to Peter and is expanding on why he was so wrong in reverting to a kosher diet while still at Antioch. So it is an absurdity to understand verse 16, with its thrice-repeated "works of law," as meaning that Paul suddenly started arguing with Peter about how wrong it was to try to base one's salvation on a perfect keeping of the law. But to understand these words in verse 16 as representing the false notion of how a Jew felt his Jewishness gave him a special standing with God would make verse 16 highly pertinent both to Gentile Christians at Antioch who had once felt compelled to become Jewish and to the Galatians whom the Judaizers were now compelling to become Jewish by being circumcised (cf. 6:12). Both these audiences needed to hear the Old Testament proof from Psalm 143:2 that all peoples, regardless of what cultural distinctives they possessed, were equally guilty before God, so that salvation for everyone comes from looking entirely away from anything they are in themselves and placing their confidence entirely in what God promises to do for them in Christ.

Another consideration is that the antithesis to the emphasis on believing in Christ in verse 16 is not only "works of law," but also verse 15's idea that, unlike a Gentile sinner, a Jewish sinner would be forgiven. The probability is higher that verse 15 provides the meaning for the thrice-repeated "works of law" in verse 16. We would have to regard Paul as speaking very awkwardly if we construed him as erecting *two* distinct antitheses to believing in Christ in vv. 15, 16a (Jews by nature; and works of law) before coming to the main clause in the middle of verse 16. So "works of law" was Paul's way of designating the Jewish legalistic attitude which depended upon one's Jewishness to give one a standing before God that Gentiles could never have, unless they were willing to become Jews.

A third consideration comes from the "even we" by which Paul finally introduces the main clause in v. 16b. This second mention of the "we" reminds the reader of the meaning implied by the first mention of the "we" at the beginning of verse 15. There it meant Paul and Peter as Jews because of the words, "We [although we were] Jews by nature ..." Now with the pronoun "we" again explicitly stated in the Greek and given an intensive force by the και ("even"), the meaning is that "even we Jews, despite our Jewish distinctives, have simply believed in Christ Jesus in order to be righteous before God and have not depended at all on these distinctives 'works of law' for this standing." Since v. 16a's negation of the "works of law" comes in between these two "we"s, so that Paul discounts the value of Jewish advantages as vehemently in v. 16b as he did in v. 15, it is difficult to agree with Bruce that "not by works of law" means that "the Jew or the Gentile now stands before God as a human being ... to be given a status before him not by legal works, in which the Jew would have an [*at least theoretical*] advantage, but on a basis [the faithfulness of Christ] equally open to Jew and Gentile (cf. Romans 3:28–30) [italics added] (p. 138)." But if "works of law" is introduced here to negate both Jews' and Gentiles' attaining a status before God by "legal works," then Paul should not have bracketed the first mention of "works of law" by the two "we"s, whose purpose is expressly to deny validity precisely to the Jewish sense of superiority. Instead he should have put "works of law" in a context like Romans 3:22 f., where his intention was to affirm that "there is no distinction, for all have sinned and come short of the glory of God." Then too, it is difficult to think how Paul could ever have thought that Jews had "an [at least theoretical] advantage" over a Gentile in achieving a status before God by "legal works." His use of Psalm 143:2 denies *all* such advantage to anyone, including a Jew.

A fourth consideration is found in the positive reason Paul affirms for putting his faith in Jesus: "because we knew that a person is ... justified ... through the faithfulness of Jesus Christ, even we have believed in Christ Jesus." Since the Reformation many scholars have rendered the nominal genitive phrase δια πιστεως Ιησου Χριστου as an objective genitive phrase, in which Jesus is the object of faith, equivalent to the verbal genitive phrase εις Χριστον Ιησουν επιστευσαμεν (we believed in Christ Jesus). Aside from the fact that when πιστις occurs in a phrase with a personal noun, it almost always indicates the faith(fulness) of the person, Paul's desire in this sentence is to give contrasting grounds for why he and the other apostles put their faith in Jesus (the main clause in this verse): the negative ground is "works of law," and the positive ground is "the faithfulness of Jesus Christ." The rhetorical power of this contrasting construction makes the main clause stand out more vividly.

Note. In understanding "works of law" as Paul's term to express the sin of the legalism involved in the Jewish confidence that their sins, unlike the Gentiles', would be forgiven, we do not mean to say that this is a sin that only Jews count. In Romans 3:20 Paul uses the term, also in a rewording of Psalm 143:2, to support the conclusion, reached in verse 19, "that every mouth may be stopped, and all the world may be held accountable to God." Here Paul's thinking is that all peoples of earth pride themselves in their cultural heritages and like to think that their particular ideals and distinctive modes of behavior make them superior to other peoples and consequently more favored by God, or the gods. Thus, in order to show that no people can claim exoneration and special blessing from God on such bases, he says in verse 20, "For by works of law shall no flesh be justified in his sight." At the beginning of verse 19, he had said that the law was given to Israel, in order that every mouth may be stopped, etc. The thought is that Israel's misuse of the law, in thinking of it as giving them a special advantage, is the reason for the calamities that have befallen her (cf. Deuteronomy 29:21–28; and Ezekiel 5:5–12). It is from these calamities that all nations should learn to avoid committing the sin represented by the term "works of law."

Note. For an answer to the objection that the nearest phrase to "works of law" in Judaism meant the righteousness of doing everything commanded by the law (and not the sin of legalism) see my *Gospel and Law: Contrast or Continuum?*, pp. 89–97. Here you'll find the extended argument for regarding "works of law" as sinful works from such verses as Romans 7:5, 13, where sin takes occasion by any law to use that law as a means of ultimate self-glorification, so that the works of law do involve one's being sinful beyond measure. This is the sense of "through the law is the knowledge of sin" [Romans 3:20b; 7:7, 8], and not covenant theology's idea that the law convicts a person of his/her sinfulness, so that one gives up all effort to be saved by obeying the law, and turning away from it, finds forgiveness in the gospel instead.

Surely the law never convicted Paul of his sins, for before the Damascus road he was, as touching the law, blameless, (Philippians 3:6). But nevertheless his sinfulness had used the good, holy, righteous, and spiritual law (Romans 7:12, 14) to make him as the chief of sinners "sinful beyond measure" during all the time he thought he was blameless. For a somewhat shorter discussion of the nature of the Mosaic Law and the phrase "works of the law," see the Appendix at the end of this work.

2:17 But if while seeking to be justified in Christ we ourselves have also been found to be sinners, is Christ then one who encourages sin? Absolutely not!

This verse presents an objection to what Paul has just said in 2:15–16. The objection was that if Paul and Peter, in seeking to be justified by Christ (17a), had to regard themselves as no better than sinners of the Gentiles (cf. 2:15) by denying any worth to Jewish distinctives for giving them an advantage with God (17b), then they were making Christ work for sin's advantage (17c). In other words, by removing all the righteousness which Jews had always claimed they had in comparison with Gentile sinners, Christ was really increasing sin by discounting all the Jews' righteousness. So the teaching of Peter and Paul about Christ was false, for the same Christ could not at the same time be increasing sin, and yet diminishing it by justifying people. Paul answers this objection, stated as a question, with a μη γενοιτο, "Perish the thought." In showing why this objection is absurd in the verses that follow Paul argues (cf. the γαρ introducing v. 18) for the thesis of 2:15–16, namely, that "a person is justified, not by works of the law, but by the faithfulness of Christ."

2:18 But if I build up again those things I once destroyed, I demonstrate that I am one who breaks God's law.

Bruce lists the *first* possible meaning of "building up what had been torn down" as "Peter's attempt to rebuild the social partition between Jews and Gentiles which he had earlier broken down" (p. 142). But then Bruce denies that this clause refers to any such specific situation. In keeping with his decision to regard "works of law" as trying to attain justification by keeping the law perfectly, Bruce understands

Paul's meaning here to be that "anyone who, having received justification through faith in Christ, thereafter reinstates the law in place of Christ makes himself a sinner all over again" (p. 142). But if this is what this argument is saying, it would have been useless in silencing the objector of v. 17. For Paul to support his utter rejection of this objection, he has to say more than "to the contrary, I become a sinner again if I forsake Christ and try to keep the law perfectly." The Jew who voiced the objection of v. 17 would say, "Not so, Paul. For if you would return to Judaism and regard yourself as a sinner who, unlike the Gentiles, will be saved, there doesn't need to be any talk of your being righteous only if you keep the law perfectly, for Judaism points to numerous ways that Jews can be forgiven." The great authority on Judaism, G. F. Moore in his three-volume work, *Judaism*, 1927, lamented the proneness of Protestants to forget that forgiveness, on the basis of repentance, is very central to Jewish thinking" (I, pp. 507, 521).

So we must construe Paul quite differently in 2:18. Paul shifts from the "we" to the "I," to indicate, as said above, that Peter was now to be regarded as standing with Paul against the Judaizers at Galatia. At this point Paul does not indicate how Peter's action constituted a transgression of the law. But at Galatians 3:8, where "works of law" had appeared before (3:2,5) and afterwards (3:10), Paul alludes to Genesis 12:3 and affirms that *because* God would bless all nations in Abraham's seed, *therefore* all peoples (including Jews) would be justified by faith. A parallel passage in Romans 3:28–30 comes to the same conclusion but appeals to the Shema ("Hear, 0 Israel, the Lord our God is one" — Deuteronomy 6:4) as a further supporting argument. So, according to the law itself, there is only one God (Deuteronomy 6:4), and this one God is the God of all the peoples of all the earth (Genesis 12:3). So if he is equally the God of all peoples, then he will bless them because they put their trust in him. This blessing could not be on the basis of any cultural distinctives, for that would make God more the God of one people than another. So Paul argues that the promise of Genesis 12:3, "In your seed shall all the nations bless themselves," necessarily implies the Gospel message that all nations receive justification through faith. Now it becomes evident how Paul, or anyone for that matter, would *transgress* the Shema and Genesis 12:3, by saying that God, on the basis of one set of cultural distinctives, prefers one ethnic group over the rest of the peoples of earth.

2:19 For through the law I died to the law so that I may live to God

Paul has now overcome the objection of v. 17 by showing that anyone inclined to make such an objection is himself a transgressor, in that he or she is undermining the very foundation of the law. The γαρ introducing v. 19 supplies an argument for the implication of v. 18 that Paul himself is certainly no transgressor of the law, *because* through the intended meaning of the revelatory law, he died to the legalism involved in the Jewish distortion of the law, so that he might live to God. As in every construction of Paul's use of νομος, so here these opposite meanings given to the same word appearing twice in the sentence is demanded by the immediate context of v. 18. There the legalistic use of "law" appeared in the idea of a Jew's building up again his cultural distinctives to give him an advantage over the Gentiles, and the revelatory use of "law" appeared in the idea of becoming a transgressor of the law. In his Pharisaic days, Paul was such a transgressor, but through regeneration and union with Christ (v. 19c), his proud heart was humbled so that he was willing to see that the gospel of salvation by faith for all peoples was at the very foundation of the law (Deuteronomy 6:4; Genesis 12:3). (Apart from such regeneration, the Jews' hearts remain hardened, and a veil, as it were, is over their eyes so they cannot see what the law is saying, because pride keeps them from it —2 Corinthians 3:14 f.)

2:20 I have been crucified with Christ, and it is no longer I who live, but Christ lives in me. So the life I now live in the body, I live because of the faithfulness of the Son of God, who loved me and gave himself for me.

Here Paul elaborates on the change effected in him through union with Christ. The proud, self-confident "I" no longer controls Paul's will. Rather, Christ controls his life by living in him (through the Holy Spirit). But Paul still retains his identity. He deliberately takes each step in life from the incentive offered by the confidence that the Christ who loved him so much as to die for him will continue to do the most benevolent things for him for the rest of his future as he is careful to obey Christ and thus maintain the joy of fellowship with him.

2:21 I do not set aside God's grace, because if righteousness could come through the law, then Christ died for nothing!

In this way the revelatory law, which expresses nothing but God's mercy and grace (and knows nothing of how a person should try to merit blessings from God — Romans 3:27; 9:31, 32a), enables Paul to live for God in the sense of doing what is pleasing to God (see the *hina* clause of v. 19). By letting the gracious, revelatory law control him so that he lives for God in a way that pleases him, Paul does not transgress the law by making it into a law of works instead of a law of faith (Romans 9:31, 32a). The Jews, to the contrary, have distorted it into a law of works. But if righteousness (both justification and sanctification) were to come through submission to this legalistic distortion of the law, then all God's grace and love that was behind Christ's dying for the world is in vain, for people are then trying to respond to God in a way that is totally contrary to God's purpose to commend his love toward them on the terms of mercy and grace, which exclude any thought of deserving God's favor. So the "law," mentioned here, through which righteousness cannot come, must be the law to which Paul died in v. 19. That was the "law" through which Paul had tried to be righteous in his pre-conversion days, but had succeeded only in being the chief of sinners. The law which brought about this death, however, was one and the same with Christ, with whom Paul was crucified at his conversion (v. 19c). Paul is not talking about that law in v. 21.

Galatians 3:1–18

3:1–5 You foolish Galatians! Who has cast a spell on you? Before your eyes Jesus Christ was vividly portrayed as crucified! ⁷ The only thing I want to learn from you is this: Did you receive the Spirit by doing the works of the law or by believing what you heard? ³ Are you so foolish? Although you began with the Spirit, are you now trying to finish by human effort? ⁴ Have you suffered so many things for nothing?— if indeed it was for nothing. ⁵ Does God then give you the Spirit and work miracles among you by your doing the works of the law or by your believing what you heard?

With the words "You foolish Galatians" in the vocative case, Paul speaks directly to his readers in a way that echoes 1:6. Ever since 2:11, and particularly in 2:15–21, he used theological reasoning to persuade his readers to maintain their allegiance to him and his teaching. (In 1:6–2:10 Paul had sought to diminish the lure the Judaizers had for the Galatians largely by a reminder of the unassailable evidence that he was an apostle of Jesus Christ [cf. 1:1].) The theological reasoning in 2:15–21 was in very concentrated form. But perhaps Paul then realized that his readers were in a bewitched and foolish state of mind and not able yet to grasp such complexity. So he now addresses then in a way suited to shake them out of their trance-like state (3:1). In 3:2 ff. he tries to focus their attention simply on one fact from their past religious experience and use it as a the starting point for the more extended theological argument of 3:6–4:11.

3:1 "Oh foolish Galatians." The "Oh" indicates the urgency with which Paul was speaking and indicates his conviction that his readers are on the brink of catastrophe. The mood of foolishness that had overtaken them is akin to that of being under a spell of witchcraft. To bring them to their senses Paul tries to direct their attention away from the Judaizers, represented by τις, back to Jesus Christ, whom Paul had "placarded" before their eyes as crucified. Only when they renounced the legalistic teaching of the Judaizers and came back to the teaching in which the cross of Christ was central would they know justification before God and be in line for the final state of righteousness that would come only through God's work (cf. 5:4).

3:2 To start them thinking again in concert with Christ as crucified, Paul directs their attention back to something they all could easily remember from their earliest Christian experience: they received the Holy Spirit through a decision involving only "a hearing of faith" and totally opposite from the decision the Judaizers were urging them to make and which Paul characterizes as "works of law." In 2:16 Paul had contrasted "works of the law" with the faithfulness of Christ leading to "faith in Christ." Since the word for "hearing," ακοης, can often be a metonymy for "what is heard," we construe this phrase here to mean exercising faith in Christ as proclaimed in the gospel. In such a decision one's attention is directed away from oneself to what God has done and promises to do. In our consideration of "works of law" in 2:16, we argued that Paul used this phrase to denote a decision by which one attains confidence of a better standing with God because of some distinction in one's person that he or she has succeeded in attaining. The Galatians could well remember that they received the blessing and joy of the Holy Spirit not by looking to something they were or had become in themselves, but rather by entrusting themselves to Christ, about whom they had heard in Paul's preaching of the Gospel.

3:3 The answer to the question posed in v. 2 was so obvious that Paul did not bother to state it. He was sure the readers would be saying, at the end of verse 2, that they had initially received the Holy Spirit not by "works of law" but by faith in Christ. So their Christian lives began in an attitude of faith, with which alone God is fully pleased and in which they enjoyed the unmatched blessing of being indwelt by the Holy Spirit. In other words, from the beginning of their Christian lives and until recently, they had enjoyed the ultimate of God's blessings. Now Paul is able to show why he was justified in declaring them to be foolish and bewitched. Only sheer foolishness would cause people to turn away from this ultimate blessing maintained simply by exercising faith, and turn toward the flesh — which urges us to exercise self-reliance. Wisdom and sober thinking will say that those who commenced their Christian lives in the enjoyment of the Holy Spirit, God's best blessing, should leave well enough alone and not try to improve on the best by supplementing in any way what is involved in living in the sphere of what the faithful Son of God accomplished on the cross. This point, the implied answer to the rhetorical question of

3:3, is the conclusion of 3:1–4:11. It reappears in different wording in 3:7, 9, 14, 24 f., 29; and 4:7.

Note: F. F. Bruce says, "The antithesis between law and Spirit [in Paul] was as absolute as the antithesis between works and faith" (p. 151). Such a statement disregards Romans 9:31, 32a, where compliance with the law was to be gained by faith, and 1 Thessalonians 1:3 and 2 Thessalonians 1:11, where Paul speaks of the "works of faith." (Cf. Romans 1:5, where Paul speaks of "the obedience of faith.") It also disregards Romans 8:4, where Paul declares that the Holy Spirit enables one to fulfill the righteous requirement of the law, and Galatians 5:22–23, where after listing the fruits of the Spirit, Paul declares that these produce no clash with the commands of the law. This observation illustrates once more how our understanding of Paul and Galatians hinges upon understanding the term "works of law."

3:6-9 [6] Just as Abraham believed God, and it was credited to him as righteousness, [7] so then, understand that those who believe are the sons of Abraham. [8] And the scripture, foreseeing that God would justify the Gentiles by faith, proclaimed the gospel to Abraham ahead of time, saying, "All the nations will be blessed in you." [9] So then those who believe are blessed along with Abraham the believer.

Again Paul is concerned to emphasize that the faith by which the Galatians began the Christian life is the same as the faith by which they proceed toward the goal of a complete, actualized righteousness (2:16, 20; 3:2, 3). Only here he reverses things by linking up a statement concerning sanctification (v. 5) with one concerning justification (v. 6, quoting Genesis 15:6) by saying "*just as* Abraham believed God, and it was counted to him for righteousness." As a consequence, in **verse 7** the Galatians should know that simply by having begun, and by continuing the Christian life, by faith, they all belong to that company of the heirs of Abraham, who will receive the blessings of Abraham. We note that virtually this same thesis is repeated in verse 9, "So that those who are of faith are blessed along with the believing Abraham." This indicates that Paul realized that the conclusion of **verse 7** could not, in the situation at Galatia, stand without further support.

There is likelihood that the Judaizers would have said in response to it, "Yes, but Abraham and his descendants had to receive circumcision to be in line for Abraham's blessing, for Genesis 17:14 says that 'any uncircumcised male ... shall be cut off from his people; he has broken my covenant." So Paul introduces in **verse 8** an additional argument drawn from Genesis 12:3 (cf. 18:18): "In you [Abraham] all the nations will be blessed." Paul argues that this statement carries with it the necessary implication that every nation would be justified by faith. The condition for receiving justification could not consist of something, like circumcision, that would make it easier for Jews than for Gentiles to be justified. It had to consist rather in faith (a condition equally easy and difficult for all). In 2:18 (above) we saw how Romans 3:28–30 joined in the argument that the Lord is the one God of all peoples (cf. Deuteronomy 6:4, the Shema), so that anyone who set forth the law as something other than a part of God's gracious love extended equally for all peoples committed the greatest transgression against the law. Now, with the argument from Genesis 15:6 (v. 6) that Abraham was blessed on account of his faith, plus the argument from Genesis 12:3 (v. 8) that faith was the way Abraham and all nations would be blessed, Paul could reaffirm the conclusion of verse 7 in **3:9**, "Consequently, those of faith will be blessed along with the believing Abraham." Συν τω πιστω Αβρααμ translated in keeping with Genesis 15:6 (v. 6) yields "believing Abraham" rather than "faithful Abraham" as in Sirach 44:20. The blessing received by all people who believe is based on justification and is topped off with the unmatched blessing of having God as one's own God (Genesis 17:7).

3:10 For all who rely on doing the works of the law are under a curse, because it is written, "Cursed is everyone who does not keep on doing everything written in the book of the law."

The thesis established in 3:3, 7, and 9 now receives further support by proving from the Old Testament that those who try to gain acceptance with God in that opposite way from faith, designated by Paul as "works of law," receive a curse, the opposite from a blessing. Bruce rejects the interpretation that "works of law" here stands for a legalistic misinterpretation of the law. He concedes that "it might well seem to follow from the language of Deuteronomy 27:26 that everyone who does persevere in doing all that the law prescribes is immune from the curse pronounced on the law-breaker" (p. 160), and should have the blessing rather than the curse spoken of in 3:10a. But "Paul's confrontation with the risen Christ on the Damascus road after his grounding in Judaism ... compelled him to see the legal path to salvation closed by a barrier (which he would not have refused to identify with the cross) which carried a notice reading: 'No road this way'" (p. 160). He quotes E. P. Sanders with approval, who interprets 3:10 to contain within it the unstated affirmation that "no one can keep the law perfectly" (E. P. Sanders, *Daube FS*, p. 106). To the objection that Judaism never insisted on a perfect keeping of the law, since it provided a number of ways in which the forgiveness of sin might be obtained, Bruce answers that Christian Jews (and presumably the Judaizers at Galatia) regarded all such methods of forgiveness as replaced by the atonement of Christ. The one great objection, however, which Bruce's interpretation of this verse leaves unanswered, is how a conclusion that Paul reached, by virtue of his Damascus road experience, was supposed to silence the Judaizers argument for the necessity of circumcision. Far to be preferred, therefore, is the interpretation which regards those of "works of law" as being the ultimate transgressors of the Old Testament law as it stands. We have argued at 2:18 and 3:8 that Genesis 12:3 and Deuteronomy 6:4 (the Shema) forbid any reliance on Jewish distinctives for acceptance with God, for such a reliance denies, in effect, that God is the God of *all* nations.

3:11 Now it is clear no one is justified before God by the law, because the one who is righteous by faith will live.

Bruce agrees that the term "works of law" of verse 10 is now represented by the abbreviated "law." This verse continues the line of thought begun in 3:10 that those of "works of law" can expect no blessing from God, but only a curse. Here Habakkuk 2:4 proves this by saying that only "he who is righteous by faith shall live." For Paul Habakkuk 2:4, along with Genesis 15:6, were the proof texts to show that justification came only by faith, whereas Psalm 143:2 (Galatians 2:16) was the proof text to show that no one could be justified by "works of law."

3:12 But the law is not based on faith, but the one who does the works of the law will live by them.

Here Paul uses the words of Leviticus 18:5 as proof that the "law" spoken of in 3:11 is not of faith. Bruce understands "law" here, as in the preceding two verses, to be the revelatory law which itself has a legalistic meaning. He says, "True, in the context of Leviticus 18:5 the promise of life to those who do what God commands is a genuine promise, but in Romans 10:5 as well as in Galatians 3:12 Paul indicates that, with the coming of the gospel, that way to life has now been closed, even if once it was open — and it is doubtful if he would concede even that [his Damascus-road experience had shown him the incompetence of the way of law-keeping and the power of the way of faith]" (p.163). Earlier he said, "Law and faith are unrelated: the gospel calls for faith, but the law requires works" (p. 162). We construe 3:12 differently from Bruce. Because of the contextual demands of "works of law" in 2:16 and ever since, we have assigned to this term a legalistic meaning never intended by the revelatory law itself. So we understand v. 12's reference to the "law" still to be a reference to the legalistic misunderstanding of the law. Beginning with the contrastive conjunction "but" (αλλα), Paul uses the wording of Leviticus 18:5 here to declare that the legalistic misunderstanding of the law is "not of faith." While he does not cite Moses as he does in Romans 10:5, his purpose is the same: to show that the righteousness of faith is the very righteousness set forth in the revelatory law.

The decisive arguments, then, for understanding "law" or "works of law" as a legalistic perversion of the revelatory law in 3:10–12 come from the exegesis of 2:16 and from our not having to insert a whole sentence in the middle of 3:10 in order for it to make sense, as Bruce, following the way Schoeps understands 3:10, is required to do. Betz declares that this way is not satisfactory (p. 146). "Paul not only fails to say what Schoeps thinks is self evident, but in fact he says the opposite [in declaring, for example, that he kept the law blamelessly, Philippians3:6–8]. The law was given to generate sin; sin is not the result of man's inability to keep [the law] ..." (pp. 145 f.).

3:13 [13] Christ redeemed us from the curse of the law by becoming a curse for us (because it is written, "Cursed is everyone who hangs on a tree")

Several questions need to be answered in this verse. Why does the law bring a curse upon people? We have seen how "works of law" appear in that attitude in which Jews regard themselves as not sinners of the Gentiles (2:15). Such an attitude undermines the very foundation of the law, which is that God is the God of all nations and wants to bless all. Thus God's anger in the form of a curse comes upon people for twisting the righteous law so that it seems to justify their thinking that they are superior to others. The Jews are by no means the only people who bring down God's curse upon themselves for this way of mishandling God's law. According to Romans 1:32–2:1, all people, despite their deep involvement in sins, know these sins to be worthy of death, even though they try to keep this knowledge out of their consciousness. That everyone thus possesses a knowledge of the law is proven by observing how prone people are to judge others for wrongdoing, even though they do the same thing themselves. Thus throughout the human race the law, consisting in the inherent sense of the wrongness of certain deeds, causes rifts between people as one group feels itself superior to others. This law then brings its own curse upon people in that God's wrath is aroused against them for using his law, not to repent and be reconciled to one another, but to set others at naught and to boast of their righteousness and ability to judge others. Christ redeems people from the wrath of God's curse against them for thus abusing and disobeying the law by himself becoming one subject to God's wrath. Paul does not elaborate here on how Jesus atoned for sin in being crucified; instead he simply cites Deuteronomy 21:23 to affirm that in that Christ was hung on a tree to die, he was under God's curse or wrath.

> **3:14** in order that in Christ Jesus the blessing of Abraham would come to the Gentiles, so that we could receive the promise of the Spirit by faith.

Jews like Paul and Peter, to whom Christ's being a curse for them had become effectual, tore down those ways in which they had used the law to keep themselves separate from the Gentiles, and they both took stands in the early church to remove the impediments of diet and circumcision from the Gentile mission, so that Paul could declare to all peoples that simply on the basis of faith they became heirs to all the spiritual blessings of Abraham. They received the forgiveness of sins, as did Abraham (Genesis 15:6). Furthermore, God became their God in the sense that all that God is as God he was for their benefit (Genesis 17:8; cf. 24:27). But all that God is as God is summed up in the Holy Spirit, for he is the personification of the love that God has for himself (Romans 5:5). So 3:14 comes back to the thesis laid down in 3:3 and repeated in 3:7 and 9, viz., that the Galatians, in beginning their Christian life in the Holy Spirit, had enjoyed God's greatest blessing; thus it was foolish of them to revert to some works of self reliance to put themselves in a position to receive God's very best.

3:15–18 [15] Brothers and sisters, I offer an example from everyday life: When a covenant has been ratified, even though it is only a human contract, no one can set it aside or add anything to it. [16] Now the promises were spoken to Abraham and to his descendant. Scripture does not say, "and to the descendants," referring to many, but "and to your descendant," referring to one, who is Christ. [17] What I am saying is this: The law that came four hundred thirty years later does not cancel a covenant previously ratified by God, so as to invalidate the promise. [18] For if the inheritance is based on the law, it is no longer based on the promise, but God graciously gave it to Abraham through the promise.

In the preceding section, 3:1–14, Paul has advanced the thesis that having the blessing of Abraham (vv. 7, 9, 14a) consists of enjoying the fullness of God's blessing of being indwelt by the Holy Spirit (w. 3, 14b) — this blessing comes to all peoples simply through faith. His arguments used to support this thesis were the Galatians' own experience of being blessed simply by faith (3:2, 5), and Genesis 12:3 and 15:6 (3:6, 8). That this blessing comes by faith and not by its opposite, "works of law," was supported by Deuteronomy 27:26 (3:10) and Hab. 2:4 (3:11). In 3:15–18, Paul affirms this thesis again by the negative statement that the law, which came 430 years after Abraham, could not nullify the promise made to Abraham and his seed, that the blessing of Abraham, or the fullness of the Holy Spirit, comes simply through trusting God (3:17). Paul's line of argument in this section is that since human oaths cannot be modified in any way (once they have been made), then how much more impossible would it be for God's oath to Abraham to be modified by any subsequent statement.

Paul seems to be saying in this paragraph that the Mosaic law, given 430 years after God ratified his promises to Abraham, cannot have modified that Abrahamic covenant in any way (w. 15, 17). Because Paul makes the strong antithesis between "law" and "promise" in v. 18, we must therefore construe his meaning of "the law" in v. 17 to have a thought-structure very opposite from that of the promise to Abraham. But to say this brings us into conflict with our interpretation of 2:19–21, which held that the *revelatory* law's intended meaning, as given at Sinai, was altogether at one with Christ and faith, in that both worked in perfect harmony to cause Paul to die to his *legalistic* understanding of the Mosaic law.

It is impossible, however, to think that Paul would affirm a difference between the Mosaic covenant and the Abrahamic in combating his opponents at Galatia. The Judaism of his day did not believe there was any difference between the Mosaic law and the Abrahamic covenant. According to 2 Baruch 57:2, "... the unwritten law was named among [Abraham, Isaac, and Jacob], and the works of the commandments was then fulfilled." Likewise, according to Kiddushin 4:14 in the Mishnah, "We find that Abraham our father had performed the whole Law before it was given, for it is written [Genesis 26:5], 'Because that Abraham ... kept my [God's] charge, my commandments, my statutes, and my laws'." From such citations, Strack-Billerbeck conclude that in the old Rabbinic understanding, "All promises were made to Abraham exclusively on the basis of his having lived righteously according to the law" (Str.-B., III, 204). So Paul would have scored no points against the Judaizers at Galatia by trying to say that he was getting his arguments from the Abrahamic covenant which could never be modified, while the Judaizers were getting their arguments from the Mosaic covenant which had no power at all to overrule the terms of the covenant God had made with Abraham.

Why then does Paul speak of the Mosaic law as though its teaching had an essential difference from that of the Abrahamic covenant, when neither he nor his adversaries believed that such a difference existed? The answer seems to be that Paul believes that with the verses he has quoted thus far, he has succeeded in proving that Abraham's righteousness was attributed to him simply because he trusted God to work for him in keeping his promises, and not at all because he distinguished himself from others through action he could boast about before God. But realizing that his opponents have construed Abraham through the lens of their misunderstanding of Moses, he then, for argument's sake, speaks of the law given by Moses as though it were different from what he has proven to be true about Abraham. The point of verse 17, then, is that even if the revelation given 430 years after Abraham taught the legalism so deeply rooted in Jewish thinking, it would not change the basis upon which Abraham attained righteousness, for this was confirmed to Abraham by an oath, and everyone knows that an oath cannot be modified once it is ratified. Such an understanding of 3:15–18 is confirmed, it seems, from verse 18, where Paul draws a sharp contrast between the "law" as the Judaizers understood it (legalism), and the promise which he believes he has made unmistakably clear from the Genesis passages. Paul believes that his readers, if not the opponents at Galatia, are convinced, both from their own experience (3:2, 5) and from passages quoted from scripture (3:6-14), that the inheritance comes by a principle of *promise* whose correlate is *faith*. As such "the promise" is a principle that is completely the opposite from the "law" (legalism) of the Judaizers. So Paul can say with confidence in verse 18 that (a) legalism and promise are two very opposite principles, and (b) that Abraham received the inheritance by promise (and not at all by any legalistic exercise).

Galatians 3:19–4:11

3:19–20 [19] Why then was the law given? It was added for the sake of transgressions, until the arrival of the descendant to whom the promise had been made. It was administered through angels by an intermediary. [20] Now an intermediary is not for one party alone, but God is one. [Fuller]

The question of v. 19, introduced by the interrogative pronoun τι, could either be a "what" or a " why" question. The answer to this question in the remainder of v. 19 tells of the purpose for which the law was given, and so we understand the question to be, "Why then the law?" The understanding of just why this question needed to be raised depends on how one construes v. 17's statement that the law coming 430 years after Abraham in no wise modified the promise made to Abraham. According to the interpretation given above, it is natural to ask: Why should God give a law to Moses when its terms in no way modified the promise he made to Abraham? (On the other hand, those like Bruce, who understand v. 17 to mean that the Mosaic law has a very different message from the Abrahamic promise, will see the question as rising out of the need to understand why something so different from the Abrahamic promise needed to be given 430 later when it could not change that promise at all.)

The answer to "Why then the law?" is that it "was added for the sake of (χαριν) transgressions." Χαριν always has a purposive meaning, and so the answer is that God added the law to his redemptive program in order to increase transgressions. In vv. 22–24 it will become clear how this penultimate work, evil in itself (God's "strange work"), will function to enhance God's ultimate and "proper work" (Luther) of abundantly blessing the sinner who believes in Jesus Christ. We note that Paul's speaking here of the law as being "added" conforms to a similar statement in Romans 5:20, "The law came in alongside in order that the trespass might abound." Betz notes (p. 165, n. 32) that Burton was the last major commentator to understand this answer to mean that the law was given to facilitate "the recognition of the sinfulness of deeds, which otherwise might have passed without recognition" (p. 188). But Bruce still draws heavily on this understanding of "for the sake of transgressions." He says, "That the promulgation of specific enactments creates a corresponding category of specific violations, with opportunity (and perhaps temptation) to commit these violations, is a fact of human experience. But Paul goes beyond this." Bruce adds, "The *purpose* of the law was to increase the sum-total of transgression" (p. 175). Bruce says very little about how the law accomplishes this surprising function, but in making this statement he does go beyond Burton and acknowledges that the law was also given for this purpose. This was surely a part of Paul's thinking, not only because of the Romans 5:20 statement (cited above) but also because in Romans 7:13 he said that "through the law sin became sinful beyond measure," and this surely means that the law's purpose was to increase sin (or transgression).

This reason for why the law was given views the law from the perspective of the law's being inferior to the promise. The rest of v. 19 cites two further aspects of the law which puts it in this inferior perspective. The law was only temporary: "It was added ... until the seed should come to whom the promise had been made." We defer until vv. 23f. a consideration of the sense in which Christ's coming set the law aside. Finally, the statement (v. 19c, 20) that the law was mediated through angels and did not come directly from the one God, as did the promise, points up the law's inferiority in still another way.

3:21–22 [21] Is the law therefore opposed to the promises of God? Absolutely not! For if a law had been given that was able to give life, then righteousness would certainly have come by the law. [22] But the scripture imprisoned everything and everyone under sin so that the promise could be given — because of the faithfulness of Jesus Christ — to those who believe.

Such derogatory talk about the law in vv. 19–20 could lead very easily to the conclusion that the nature of the law is inferior to that of the promise and therefore is at odds with the promise. Paul poses this plausible conclusion as a question which he then answers with μη γένοιτο, "Perish the thought!" He supports this vehement denial with the affirmation that "if a law was given which could make [people] alive, then righteousness certainly would have come by the law." So, according to Paul, the one thing the law lacked, which made it inferior to the promise and useful for increasing transgressions, was its lack of power to overcome the sin which has enthralled everything, according to verse 22.

In understanding the supporting statement in the remainder of v. 21, we do well not to lose sight of those passages which show how adequate the law is for making people alive when God's power, which alone is capable of defeating sin, is acting in conjunction with the revelatory law. In our interpretation of 2:19, the law received that power for Paul through his union with Christ, so that as a result he "lived unto God." This interpretation of 2:19 has to mean that, since the law and Christ worked so hand in hand to cause him to die to the legalistic law, so that he might live to God, the revelatory law therefore is in a continuum with Christ and the gospel. To be sure, after his conversion experience God allowed Paul to be devoid of this power from time to time, so that (as Paul put it) "the very commandment which promised life proved to be death to me" (Romans 7:10; 14–25). But for the most part, the law's weakness, also mentioned in Romans 8:3, is fully overcome by those indwelt by the Holy Spirit, for in having this power they fulfill the righteous ordinance (δικαιωμα) of the law (Romans 8:4). Such people were also made alive, for in this context the mind of the Spirit was characterized as "life" rather than the "death" which characterizes the mind-set of flesh (Romans 8:6). Furthermore, the law's suitableness to make alive is implied by Paul's quotation of Deuteronomy 27:26 in Galatians 3:10b. If non-compliance with the law brings a curse, then compliance with it (made possible by regeneration) brings the opposite, namely, the blessing and life of being a son of Abraham. Paul's additional positive statements about the law in Galatians 5:14 and 22f. blend well with another positive statement about the law in Romans 7:12, 14: the "law is holy and just and good" and "spiritual."

From this evidence we argue that nothing about the law's thought-structure (e.g., its supposed "conditional" promises, Calvin, *Institutes* III,2,29) nor a difference in its content, made it useful "for the sake of transgression." Since the promise to Abraham was clearly conditional (Genesis 18:19; 22:16f.), and conditional upon keeping "[God's] commandments, statutes, and laws" (Genesis 26:5), we argue that Paul's vehement negation in v. 21 means that as far as content and thought-structure are concerned, the law and the promise are one and the same. That the law's being added increased transgressions arose from nothing distinctive about the law itself in comparison with the promise, but rather from the sin under which "the scripture boxed everything in," including the law, 3:22. This means that when the sinful Israelites were confronted with the law at Sinai, it was not God's will that the majority of them should have the regenerative power necessary to be inclined to comply with the law (Deuteronomy 29:4; 5:29; cf. Jeremiah 31:31 ff..). Confronted with this holy, good, just, and spiritual law, this "law of faith," and on account of their sinfulness, they twisted it all around into a "law of works" (Romans 9:32a; cf. 3:27), and by means of this fictitious, non-revelatory, legalistic law that their sinful natures had now entrenched in their heads, "they became sinful beyond measure" (Romans 7:13). The αλλα introducing v. 22 indicates how emphatically Paul wanted to affirm that it is sin (or, law's lack of power to prevail over sin), rather than some difference in the law's thought-structure or content, which caused the law to act against the promise by increasing transgressions. The power of sin had such a devastating effect on the revelatory law that its intended meaning was twisted all around by the sinful Jews to become a legalistic "law of works" (Romans 9:32a). In this form the law became the power of sin (1 Corinthians 15:56). Cranfield understands the nature of the sin that this powerful, legalistically-construed law produced to be that which drives people "to try to use it as a means to the establishment of a claim upon God" ("St. Paul and the Law," *SJT* 17 [1964], 46f.).

Bruce hints at this possibility for interpreting v. 22, because he cites this understanding of Cranfield's as having plausibility (p. 175). But Bruce does not interpret verse 22 in this way. As for the "scripture" which "shut up all things under sin," Bruce takes Burton's position of regarding "scripture" as "tantamount to 'the written law,' concentrated in such an uncompromising form as Deuteronomy 27:26 (quoted in v. 10, above)" (p. 180). Indeed, he concedes that when "scripture" was similarly used in verse 8, it was "practically equivalent to God" (p. 155). He also concedes that "scripture" in v. 22 could also stand for "God," since Romans 11:32 is similar to verse 22 in that it speaks of God as shutting up (συγκλειω) all peoples unto disobedience. Despite all this, Bruce understands verse 22 to mean that "the written law is the official who locks the law-breaker up in the prison-house of which sin is the jailor ... Those who come to their senses in the prison-house and recognize the hopelessness of their predicament will be the readier to embrace the promise of liberty and life: the law thus serves the interests of the promise – and of the beneficiaries of the promise" (pp. 180 f.).

Several difficulties bar the acceptance of this understanding of "scripture" in verse 22. For one thing, Bruce regards the law as "a completely different instrument, quite unrelated to the promise, [and] introduced for a distinct purpose" (p. 174). So it is jarring to the reader to hear him let law be represented by scripture in this context, where the law and promise are made antithetical to each other, and where he regards the antithesis to exist in their inherent natures and in such a way that the law would be farther from the center of the scripture than the promise. Then too, the "scripture" of v. 22 envelopes *everyone* under sin by just one action. In Romans 3:19, however, Paul speaks of law as being given only to those who are under the law, that is, the Jewish nation. To be sure, the next verse goes on to say that the guilt of Israel implies the guilt of everyone. But this conclusion does not follow as a necessary inference just from Israel's being under the law, but only after the additional events of Israel's disobedience to the law, and her consequent punishment for this disobedience viewed by all the nations (Deuteronomy 29:22–28) is taken into account. So we conclude that Bruce is wrong to understand that Mosaic law, distilled in Deuteronomy 27:26, is represented by the "scripture" of v. 22.

"Scripture" surely could be represented, by a metonymy, as something as fundamental to God's purpose in redemptive history as the shutting up of all creation under sin since Adam first sinned. But it is difficult to conceive of "scripture" as representing the law, which, in Bruce's understanding, is only that one part of scripture which affirms that there must be continued and perfect obedience to even its slightest detail, or else one is eternally condemned for even the slightest misstep. (The Jews have never thought of the law in these terms, and since such an idea was not held by the Judaizers in Galatia, 3:22 understood in these terms would have been useless in winning back to Paul the allegiance of the wavering churches at Galatia.)

The biggest difficulty, however, in Bruce's interpretation of v. 22 is that he assumes that sin's powerful presence does not have any effect upon how the Jews construed this holy, righteous, good, and spiritual law given at Sinai. But Romans 9:31–32a makes very clear that the Jews ignored the intended meaning of the revelatory law and artificially twisted it around so they could regard it as a legalistic document. It says, "Israel failed to attain the law of righteousness, because she sought it not by faith, but as if it were by works." In commenting on the "as if it were" (ὡς), the grammarian Georg Winer said, "The expression εκ πιστεως ["by faith"] denotes the objective standard; [and] ὡς εξ εργον ["as of works"], the purely subjective standard" (G. B. Winer, *Grammar of the Idiom of the New Testament*, [ETr⁷, 1897], p. 619). It was because sin had boxed everything in that the Jews at Sinai rejected the law as a law of faith, and twisted it around into a law of works to suit their sinful inclinations. To the present day Israel adheres to this subjective, fanciful interpretation of the Torah because, as Paul put it in 2 Corinthians 3:14, "[The Israelites'] minds were hardened; for to this day, when they read the old covenant the same veil remains unlifted, because only through Christ is it taken away." And so it was with Paul; only when he died with Christ (Galatians 2:19) were his eyes opened so that he then saw the Mosaic law as a law of faith. Now that Paul was supplied with the power that the law for him had hitherto lacked according to 3:21, he no longer distorted it into the legalistic law of works, as he had done when a Pharisee.

As a result of the Damascus road encounter with the risen Jesus, Paul saw that despite his complete immersion in the law both at home in Tarsus, and during his training at Jerusalem under Gamaliel, he had nevertheless been totally separated from the revelatory law (Romans 7:9), in that he was completely oblivious to seeing it as a law of faith. Only after conversion did he become conscious of the intended meaning of the law. Then he realized that with his zeal by which he had blamelessly (Philippians 3:6) kept a terribly distorted version of the law, he had succeeded only in becoming the chief of sinners (cf. 1 Timothy 1:15). He had become so sinful because he had zealously persecuted Christians for making the law's cultural distinctives nonessential by insisting that even circumcised, kosher-diet Jews could be saved only if they repented and were baptized into the name of Jesus Christ for the forgiveness of sins (Acts 2:38). Paul had gloried so in these distinctives (Philippians 3:4 ff..) that he killed Christians and laid waste the churches (Galatians 1:13). His purpose was to eradicate all Jews who, in effect, denied the value of Jewish distinctives for having a standing with God.

It has been noted that the Reformation has interpreted Paul's view of the law, not on the basis of Paul's own conversion experience (in which there was no sense of guilt prior to conversion), but on the analogy of the conversion experiences of Augustine, Luther, and Calvin — each of whom had a struggle with guilt before conversion. But their experiences are irrelevant for the understanding of Paul and the law. Understanding the law's function to be that of bringing a person to Christ by making him feel guilty and in need of the forgiveness provided by the gospel does not fit at all with what was true for Paul or for Israel, who were in the foreground of his thinking as he goes on in vv. 23f. to speak of the "we" of Israel who were shut up under law.

Before proceeding to v. 23, the purpose clause of v. 22, "in order that the promise, secured by the faithfulness of Jesus Christ, might be given to those who believe," needs to be interpreted. We construe it to declare God's final, benevolent purpose in ordaining the penultimate evil of shutting up all things under sin and then ordaining the law so that it would increase sinfulness and transgressions beyond measure. That God remains just while justifying such sinful people who believe in Jesus Christ causes his glory to stand out all the more resplendently than would have been the case had there been no sinfulness beyond measure for which people needed forgiveness.

> **3:23** Now before faith came we were held in custody under the law, being kept as prisoners until the coming faith would be revealed.

Bruce regards this verse as repeating v. 22, only in different terms. This verse, however, leaves behind v. 22's theme which embraces the whole scope of redemptive history, and focuses on one particular segment of it, namely, the period between Sinai and the Christ event. It also ceases to look at "all things" and narrows its view just to the people of Israel who, before the coming of "the faith" in the person of Christ, were being closely guarded, as it were, under law, shut up in a cell like prisoners until that faith was to be revealed. Here we notice that "law" is what boxes in the Jews: The Jewish misinterpretation of the law, brought about by sin's having boxed everything in (v. 22), is now what keeps the Jews in the miserable state of bondage (without their realizing it) of being sinful beyond measure. In the way they have misconstrued the revelatory law, they regard its precepts as part of the job description (a law of works) in which they could boast before God and thus imply that they were completely praiseworthy to him. Had they complied, however, with the intended meaning of the revelatory law, they would have understood its precepts to be like a doctor's prescription (a law of faith) in which God was working for their benefit and thereby laying a complete claim upon them to serve and worship him.

So their sinfulness beyond measure consisted in a cosmic role-reversal in which they had made God trade places with them and become the employer whom they served instead of the Workman who served them (Isaiah 64:4). Their misconstrued law, which is the power of sin (1 Corinthians 15:56), so deceived and blinded them to the truth, that the law could not possibly convict them of their sins so they would turn, as Bruce supposes, to faith in Christ. So when Christ did finally come, the law (in general) did not convict the Jews so that they would look in a different direction — toward Christ — to find forgiveness. Most Jews persisted in their false understanding of the law, and that is why Paul said that those who were under its works were under a curse. To be relieved of the curse of the works of that law (3:10), the Jews would have had to disobey their notion of the law as radically as Paul did when the revelatory law came to him on the Damascus road and he "died" in the misery of realizing his Pharisaic law had succeeded not in making him blameless but the chief of sinners instead.

From verse 23, it might seem that Jews were freed from the law with the coming of Christ, but Paul could not have meant this, for he lamented at the persistent blindness of his kinsfolk years after the conclusion of the Christ-event (Romans 9–11). Rather, the point to be made in focusing on this segment of Jewish history from Moses to Christ is to provide all nations with a lesson book detailing the disasters that befell Israel because she disobeyed God's law. According to

Ezekiel 5:5–12, Israel was placed at the center of the nations so all nations could see what horrors would befall them also if they, like Israel, should take God's grace in the law and/or the gospel, and turn it around into a doctrine of works by which they supposed they could boast before God. So the grace of God manifested in Christ, which is so much a part and parcel of God's grace in the law (John 1:16–17; Romans 9:32–33), comes in after this period of Israel's ultimate rebellion, as a warning that all such rebellious nations should not model Israel's example of misconstruing her law, but repent so that they rest their hope for an eternity of happy tomorrows on God's grace, revealed in the law and summed up in Christ. Instead of being the persons who work to display their own capabilities before God and so lay a claim upon him, they must be humble recipients of mercy and welfare, who obey God's precepts much as sick patients follow a doctor's regimen to get well and then feel so very indebted to the skill and benevolence of the doctor who knew how to heal them.

The Christ-event marks the beginning of the Gentile Mission and the carrying out of the Great Commission. The lesson to be learned from Israel's legalism is thus completely written by that time. Consequently, those matters in the law (circumcision and a kosher diet) that were most conducive to a prideful legalism and would provide insurmountable barriers against bringing the blessing of Abraham to the peoples of earth with their wide variety of cultures had to drop away as the Gentile Mission commenced. It is in this sense that the law lasts only until the Christ-event. But those features of the law that apply equally despite cultural differences continue to be in force, and so Paul can talk of the law as normative for Christians of all cultures in Romans 13:8-10 and Galatians 5:14, and even say in 1 Corinthians 7:19, "Circumcision [is] nothing, and uncircumcision [is] nothing; instead the keeping of the commandments of God [is everything]."

> **3:24** Thus the law had become our custodian until Christ, so that we could be declared righteous by faith. [Fuller]

Paul summarizes things by saying that the good law *became* the Jews' παιδαγωγος "until Christ." The emphasis in this verse, as in the preceding, on the confining purpose of the law provides the clue for understanding the crucial features of this verse. The παιδαγωγος here functions as the law in v. 23 to keep Israel closely guarded and shut up in their sins. Far from having an educative function, the good law *became* instead a harsh custodian because, as we have seen, the sinfulness of humankind, into which the good law came (3:22), changed the revelatory law, which was in every way like the promise (3:21), away from a gracious law of faith and made it into a law of works. But while this law did not prepare Israel for Christ by educating her in any way, yet the calamities which befell Israel (Deuteronomy 29:24–28; Ezekiel 5:7–12) were to educate all the nations of earth, pictured in Ezekiel 5:5 as seated around Israel. From observing the dreadful punishments God has meted out against Israel for her sacrilegious behavior of presuming to boast before God, the nations have a powerful example to teach them to respond to God instead by an obedience of faith. So according to 3:24, the good, holy, righteous, and spiritual law became a harsh prison guard, confining Israel under the miseries of sinfulness. But all this was "until Christ." That is, the law so misused by Israel provides the contrasting backdrop emphasizing the necessity of serving God through an obedience of faith, the message so consonant with the faithful Christ's incarnation, death, resurrection, and ascension.

3:25–27 [5] But now that faith has come, we are no longer under a guardian. [26] For in Christ Jesus you are all sons of God through faith. [27] For all of you who were baptized into Christ have clothed yourselves with Christ.

Then who are the "we" who are no longer under this harsh custodian? Potentially, it is the Jewish nation as a whole, for in that God proffered them forgiveness of sins, not on the basis of their distinctives, but simply if they would repent and be baptized into Jesus for the forgiveness of sins (Acts 2:38), God was saying that all their use of the law and their Jewish heritage for claiming blessings from him was ineffective, and they must come to God like "sinners of the Gentiles" (2:15). We know, however, that the great majority of Israel rejected Christ, so the law, as their slave master, continued to write the lesson book to provide the nations with additional evidence of how severely God would treat them if they, like Israel, rejected his mercy and grace in the gospel of Christ. But in actuality, "we" indicates Paul and the other Jews who believed on Jesus were released from the legalistic law and from that power of sin (cf. 1 Corinthians 15:56) which had made them sinful beyond measure. The veil had been lifted from their eyes and they complied properly with the revelatory law so that they might live unto God (cf. 2:19), and go on being saved simply by exercising faith in Jesus (cf. 3:6-9). This was the way Jews should live (3:26) *since* the Gentiles, symbolized in the Galatian readers (the "you" of verse 26), were sons of God through faith in Christ, without depending on any Jewish distinctives. In 3:8 Paul declared how it had been God's purpose all along to bless the nations of earth, and this had to mean that they would be saved by faith (an action that had nothing to do with their various distinctives). So verse 26 argues for verse 25 by saying that since the Gentiles were being saved by faith, therefore (v. 25) the Jewish believers were surely to be saved by faith and were not under the slave master. This interpretation of how verse 26 argues for verse 25 is enforced by the statement in 3:8 that God preached the gospel beforehand *to Abraham*. In other words, *because* now peoples from all the various ethnic entities of earth are being saved by faith, *therefore* the Jews must now be saved in that way too; to use the wording of Romans 3:29, 30, " ... God is one, and he will justify the circumcision on the ground of their faith, and the uncircumcised through their faith."

Jews and Gentiles are saved alike, according to 3:25–26, because (3:27) whoever has been baptized into Christ has put on Christ as the one and only distinctive that answers to what really saves a person. Just as circumcision was a valid sign only when it answered to a real righteousness (Romans 2:24; 4:11) in the wearer of that distinctive, so there is every reason to understand that Paul, when he spoke of believers' being baptized into Christ, was thinking not only of the rite of baptism, but also of the reality of being united with Christ (cf. 2:19–20).

> **3:28** There is neither Jew nor Greek, there is neither slave nor free, there is neither male nor female — for all of you are one in Christ Jesus.

This union with Christ, as symbolized by water baptism, makes people diverse in race, class, and gender all as one. Whatever distinctions exist because of these diversities, none should contribute to nor detract from the full enjoyment of the blessings of being in Christ. To be sure, this means that the slave is to enjoy the blessings of Christ as much as his master, and the woman, as much as the man. But it also means that Christians belonging to the privileged race (the Jews) or class (like the slave masters) or gender (the men) must allow this oneness in Christ to modify any traditionally-approved behavior that tends to restrict the traditionally subordinate members of these false hierarchies from enjoying all the blessings of Christ.

NOTE. The phrase "neither Jew nor Greek" required radical behavior changes that do not find their counterpart in Paul's explicit teachings echoing "neither slave nor free" and "not male and female" because all the fledgling church's energy had to be conserved for the time being in bringing Jews into line with the implications of oneness in Christ. Similarly radical changes of behavior were required of slave owners and males, but Paul accommodated himself to slavery and patriarchalism and enforced a Christianized version of them with theological sanctions, even though they were to be destroyed, one at a time, as soon as the Jew-Gentile problem was laid to rest. The way Paul enjoined Philemon to treat Onesimus meant that no Christian could own a Christian as a slave. And that Paul did not rebuke the women who prophesied in a public assembly (1 Corinthians 11:2–16), when his rule was that women are to keep silent in the church (1 Corinthians 14:34), shows that rule was a temporary accommodation and has no authority that binds us now. If every member of the body of Christ, both male and female, gets at least one spiritual gift (1 Corinthians 12:7) for the edification of the church, and if these gifts are given sovereignly "to every person even as God wills" (1 Corinthians 12:11), then we must all acquiesce in the gifts God gives to women as well as to men. It seems impossible to avoid the conclusion that those who enforce any version of the master-slave relationship (in treating their employees) and the male-female hierarchy (in regarding women as subservient to or bound to take orders from men) are also guilty of the Galatian error. In that they oppress workpeople or deny that women are as free as men to do as they feel inclined in the church or at home, they are making it impossible for other believers to have the full blessing that comes from exercising the spiritual gifts God has given them. (For a more detailed exposition of this verse see the Appendix at the end of the book.)

3:29 And if you belong to Christ, then you are Abraham's descendants, heirs according to the promise.

Now Paul draws the conclusion whose partial groundwork was laid in 3:16, where he quoted Genesis 17:7, "Now the promises were made to Abraham and to his offspring. It does not say, 'And to descendents,' referring to many; but, referring to one, 'And to your descendent,' which is Christ." But the word for "descendents" in Genesis is a singular, collective noun, which by no means singles out one individual, like Jesus Christ. The argument in Genesis is that the promise is to a group of people, characterized as Abraham's offspring, but who distinguish themselves from other groups — and even others who have Abraham as their physical father — by being those who believe God's promises. Understood in this way, the Genesis passage remains open to the supplemental knowledge, added later, that these promises would be made to that whole group of physical descendants of Abraham through One of that seed who would make it possible for God to grant such gracious promises to the rest of the group who were sinful people. Now Paul argues in verse 29 that those who are *of Christ* (that is, those who have been united with Christ through the indwelling Spirit — see 2:19f. and 3:27) are also the seed of Abraham in the normal sense that language conventions attach to the word "seed."

Since Christ himself traced his lineage back to Abraham, then all those actually united with Christ are, by virtue of that union, also the offspring of Abraham and are the inheritors of the promises made to him. So here in 3:29 Paul reiterates for the sixth time (see 3:7, 9, 14, 17, 26) the thesis of 3:1–4:11, that God's blessings (or Abraham's blessings) come to peoples of all ethnic backgrounds simply on the basis of faith in these promises. Apparently the Judaizers at Galatia had been arguing from Genesis 17:14 ("Any uncircumcised male who is not circumcised in the flesh of his foreskin shall be cut off from his people ...") that the Christians there had to submit to circumcision in order to have God's full blessing. But Paul has advanced a series of arguments that show that Genesis 17:14 had only a limited application and was not consonant with Genesis 12:3 (cf. 3:6–9).

4:1–2 Now I mean that the heir, as long as he is a minor, is no different from a slave, though he is the owner of everything. ² But he is under guardians and managers until the date set by his father.

Paul wants to support the previous thesis from still another line of argument, this time (4:1–8) borrowing from an analogy in the practice of the Roman law of that day, that an heir was under guardians and trustees for a fixed term (προςθεσμια) decided on by the father, which could last up until age twenty-five. Only at that time did the heir become his own master and have full enjoyment of the inheritance. There is difficulty in thinking that wealthy fathers wanted their sons to be treated as harshly as slaves were often treated. But an illustration does not have to support every affirmation that could be drawn from it.

4:3 So also we, when we were minors, were enslaved under the elemental spirits of the world.

Here Paul is depicting the time period between Sinai and Christ when the Jewish people were placed in bondage under the law as their sinfulness caused them totally to misinterpret it (cf. 3:22–24). The beings who answer to the "guardians and trustees" are the στοιχεια. That they should be understood as personal beings is supported (1) by their being represented by "guardians and trustees" (v. 2), and (2) by the way Paul speaks of them in verses 8–11, where they can be mistaken for gods and have the power to enslave people. Thinking of them as demons would fit in well with 3:22, where God shut up all things under sin. Demons would give sin that power before which the law, by itself, was defenseless, and from which a person could be delivered only by union with Christ. That the (majority of the) Jews were under such servitude for an extended time period is emphasized by the imperfect in the temporal clause, and by the periphrastic use of the participle, "we were being enslaved to the demonic spirits of the world" in the main clause.

4:4–5 ⁴ But when the fullness of time had come, God sent out his Son, born of a woman, born under the law, ⁵ to redeem those who were under the law, so that we may be adopted as sons with full rights. [Fuller]

That "fullness of time" which had to run its course was the centuries between Sinai and the Christ-event, during which Israel's sinfulness beyond measure in misinterpreting and thereby disobeying the law could become manifest and emphasized by the singular devastation inflicted upon the nation and its land. It took time for Israel's "lesson book" — the historical events that showed the severity God meted out against Israel for rejecting his mercy — to be assembled as the major part of the scriptures to undergird the preaching of the gospel to all peoples. In Romans 11:17-24 Paul explicitly spells out to the Gentiles how they are to fear the unbelief that caused Israel to be cast off from God like branches from a domesticated olive tree. The Gentiles are likened to branches taken from a wild olive tree and grafted into the domesticated tree nourished by roots representing the blessings God promised the patriarchs Abraham, Isaac, and Jacob. From Israel's example of unbelief the Gentiles learn God's severity, in order that they, fearing unbelief so greatly, would remain in God's kindness by trusting in his promises perseveringly. The Gentile mission would have been greatly deficient had not God allowed this "fullness of time" for the writing of Israel's lesson book for the nations.

As the law had come in under sin and had succumbed to its power as sinful hearts perverted it to a meaning that would comply with sin, so Jesus Christ, the son of God, came into the sinful world to which the perverted law had now given sin its strength (1 Corinthians 15:56). Paul's implication is that though Jesus was in the middle of this bastion of evil, he withstood it all in order to redeem people who were under its power, so that they might receive the blessing of being adopted as God's children.

> **4:6–7** [6] And because you are sons, God sent the Spirit of his Son into our hearts, who calls "Abba! Father!" [7] So you are no longer a slave but a son, and if you are a son, then you are also an heir through God.

In addition to sending Jesus into the world. God sent the Spirit of Jesus into the hearts of those who had been adopted as sons, and the proof that this was Jesus' Spirit is that God's sons address him as "Abba, Father." According to Bruce (p. 199), Αββα was "the domestic term by which a father was called in the affectionate intimacy of the family circle." Those fearfully living (cf. Romans 8:15) like slaves under the domination of the παιδαγωγος (3:24) could not be certain of receiving God's blessings. But now freed from such bondage, one looks to God as the One who deeply yearns to bestow the greatest benefits upon his beloved children. Verse 7 concludes by telling how such children are in line for the inheritance. Adoption, the spirit of sonship, and the inheritance are aspects of the fullness of blessing that believers should enjoy simply on the basis of faith, a confidence in God and his promises which leaves no room for the feelings of oppression and fear which occur when one tries to be impressive to God.

4:8–11 [8] Formerly when you did not know God, you were enslaved to beings that by nature are not gods at all. [9] But now that you have come to know God (or rather to be known by God), how can you turn back again to the weak and worthless elemental spirits? Do you want to be enslaved to them all over again? [10] You are observing religious days and months and seasons and years. [11] I fear for you that my work for you may have been in vain.

Having just drawn the contrast between the states of being a slave and of being a son, Paul asks the Galatians how they can possibly want to go back to the slavery that they had once experienced as pagans and that they would experience again if they heeded the Judaizers and submitted to circumcision. Paul understands the situation of unregenerate Israel's serving her distorted Mosaic law as being no better than that of the Galatians in their previous paganism (cf. 4:3 and 10). The argument of verses 9 ff. faintly echoes 1:6 f. How can the Galatians be so foolish as to want to turn from the position of having the one true God as their Father, back to wanting to be enslaved to demonic beings who in comparison with God are weak (cf. 3:5 where God works miracles *dunameis*) and poor (cf. 4:7 where God imparts the priceless blessings of his inheritance)? Why should they want to supplement simple trust in God's great promises with such useless things as observing days, months, seasons, and years? If they bring in anything as a supplement to faith they will commit the most terrible error — Galatianism! It is no wonder that Paul fears that all his labor for the Galatian churches may well have been in vain.

Galatians 4:12–5:1

In 4:8–11, at the conclusion of the theological argument begun at 3:1, Paul came the closest yet to speaking imperatively to the Galatians. If we restate the question of 4:9 declaratively, it reads, "There is no reason at all for your wanting to turn away from God, whom you have come to know, back *again* to become enslaved again (note how emphatically this idea is stated by the use of παλιν twice, and with ανωθεν, a synonym, the second time [seemingly impossible to represent in good English]) to the weak and impoverished demons." This implies the imperatival idea, "Do not to turn away from the God who wants to pour out his blessing on you, back to the demons who only want to abuse you."

At 4:12 Paul again speaks directly to his readers in Galatia in tones reminiscent of 1:6–7 (which introduced the biographical argument) and of 3:1–5 (which introduced his theological argument). In 4:12–20 Paul reverts to the biographical argument, only this time he goes beyond the implicit imperative of 1:6–7 and uses the first explicit imperative in Galatians: "Brethren, I beseech you, become as I am, for I have become as you are. Then in 4:21–5:1 he reverts to a theological argument based on the Ishmael-Isaac section of Genesis, and here again he utters an explicit imperative: "Stand fast therefore [in the liberty wherewith Christ has made you free], and do not submit again to the yoke of slavery" (5:lb). Explicit imperatival statements increase in frequency from now on until the epistle ends with chapter 6.

4:12 I beg you, brothers and sisters, become like me, because I have become like you.

What Paul means in imploring the Galatian brethren to "become as I am" is indicated by the causal clause, "because even I became as you are." The argument is that if Paul, in bringing the gospel to the Gentile Galatians, deliberately refrained from practicing any specifically Jewish customs, and aligned his behavior with the culture pattern of the Galatian Gentiles, then how much more should the Galatians ignore the Judaizers' plea to add some Jewish distinctives to their cultural profile and live in the *Christian* Gentile manner (cf. 2:12ff.) that Paul, the Jew, had modeled when he first evangelized them. So the first argument supporting the imperative of verse 12a is that *since* Paul, in the past, loved the Galatians enough to leave behind all his Jewish credentials, *therefore* they ought not to scorn that love, but honor it, by continuing to be controlled simply by Paul's teaching, so they can go on enjoying the priceless blessings of Abraham (3:7–8).

> **4:12c–14** You have done me no wrong! [13] But you know it was because of a physical illness that I first proclaimed the gospel to you, [14] and though my physical condition put you to the test, you did not despise or reject me. Instead, you welcomed me as though I were an angel of God, as though I were Christ Jesus himself!

The second argument (vv. 12c–20) is that he has continued until the present to have a genuine love for the Galatians that contrasts very strongly with the counterfeit love that the Judaizers express in their zeal to win over the Galatians' allegiance. The starting point for this second argument is that the Galatians did not wrong Paul when he first evangelized them (12c). (To speak of them as doing him no wrong implies how greatly, by contrast, they are now wronging him by rejecting his gospel.)

Far from wronging him then, they showed him great love when he first preached the gospel to them "on account of a bodily weakness" (δια with the accusative). Some sort of illness had caused Paul to lay over in Galatia. This weakness apparently had some loathsome aspect to it, which would ordinarily repel people. But the Galatians were so blessed by the message Paul preached that they welcomed him and his gospel as if he were an angel from God or even Christ Jesus himself. They had counted themselves fortunate/happy (μακαρισμοσ) to have such a message, even though the messenger had a repulsive sickness.

> **4:15** Where then is your sense of happiness now? For I testify about you that if it were possible, you would have pulled out your eyes and given them to me! [16] So then, have I become your enemy by telling you the truth?

But with the question, "Where has your sense of being blessed gone?" Paul indicates how the Galatians' attitude toward him has markedly changed. Once their blessing from God was so great as they complied with Paul's teaching, that they loved him enough to be willing to give him "their eyes" (that is, their most prized possession). But they no longer regard the Christian message to be all that valuable. The Judaizers have made them suspect that Paul's message was incomplete. They have also promised the Galatians an experience of God's complete blessedness if they will accept the distinctive of circumcision as necessary to that blessing. The rhetorical question, "Have I become your enemy?" conveys the meaning that they had turned from loving Paul to regarding him as a hostile threat, in spite of his telling them the truth, now as always.

> **4:17–18** They court you eagerly, but for no good purpose; they want to exclude you, so that you would seek them eagerly. ^{18} However, it is good to be sought eagerly for a good purpose at all times, and not only when I am present with you.

Paul has genuinely loved the Galatians, and continues to do so now, despite their hatred of him. This continued love, which is obliquely stated in verse 18, is the explicit statement of the second reason why the Galatians should obey the imperative of 4:12, "Become as I am." **V. 17** helps the readers understand how valuable Paul's love toward them is by showing them how unloving the apparent "love" of the Judaizers is for the Galatians. Paul was saying in effect, "The zeal (ζηλοω) by which the Judaizers pay court to you is not good. Rather, they simply want to shut you off from me and my gospel, in order that they might have you pay court to them." (How, then, could they possibly retain love for the Judaizers, when it meant (1) being cut off from the blessings of God conveyed through Paul's gospel, and (2) no longer being loved as ends, as they were under Paul's leadership, but having to serve the Judaizers' needs by paying court to them?) In v. 18 Paul declares that he, by contrast, does not just appear loving when he is with them, but has an abiding love for them whether present or absent. What then was the driving force of Paul's love for the Galatians? It was not, as with the Judaizers, that in so doing Paul would get the Galatians to pay homage to him. Paul's motivation in loving them was rather to gain the satisfaction of seeing how much others have benefitted from the blessing he has succeeded in passing along to them. It is that doubled joy of a shared joy (Goethe), or as Jesus put it, it is the greater happiness of giving rather than keeping something for oneself (Acts 20:35). So Paul does get great gain from his genuine love for the Galatians, but this gain in no wise involves his using them as means to his ends.

4:19–20 My children — I am again undergoing birth pains until Christ is formed in you! [20] I wish I could be with you now and change my tone of voice, because I am perplexed about you.

Paul then proceeds to argue that he has such love for the Galatians, for right now he is, as it were, willing to endure a mother's birth-pangs until Christ is formed in them again. And so Paul likens his love for the Galatians to that of mother-love. And by saying, "My little children," he is also likening his love for the Galatians to that of a father (cf. 1 Thessalonians 2:6-12 for a similar argument with the same metaphors). By likening his love to the most powerful expressions of it in human experience, Paul was showing the Galatians how only his love was worth responding to. We should also note that in saying he was, as it were, giving birth *again* to the Galatians, he was implying that it was at least problematical that they are now enjoying union with Christ. We recall from 2:19–20 how it was union with Christ that had killed Paul's desire to glorify his ego. But since the Galatians were responding positively to the Judaizers who had succeeded in flattering their egos, it appeared that Christ was not an integral part of their lives. Verse 20 indicates another way in which Paul's love for the Galatians is truly genuine. He wishes that he might be with them now and see them change their attitude so he would not have to speak so harshly, because he is deeply upset about them. Since Paul, unlike the Judaizers, is not loving them for the ulterior motive of getting them to pay court to him, but is loving them as ends in themselves, they should therefore become like Paul, and regard the wearing of Jewish distinctives as completely irrelevant, as Paul did when he preached the Gospel to them. Then they will regain the sense of blessedness they have known in Christ, for their only concern will again be to find fulfillment in their lives by living in accord with the faith of Christ, who loved them and gave himself up for them.

4:21 Tell me, you who want to be under the law, do you not understand the law?

Having used the personal argument to turn the Galatians away from the bondage involved in taking on Jewish distinctives (4:12–20), Paul now reverts to the theological argument. He believes that the "law," in the sense of the Pentateuch, contains an obvious warning against all who would come "under law" — the term Paul has used to indicate coming under the power of evil by responding to the law in some legalistic frame of mind (3:23; 4:4,5 [cf. 1:4]; and 5:18). In 4:21–31 Paul sets forth his message to the Galatians in terms of an "allegory" (v. 24), a figurative treatment of one subject under the guise of another. Paul's message (one thing) is now conveyed in terms of the Isaac-Ishmael narrative in Genesis (another thing). An allegory is a valid literary device when the "other terms" set forth meanings that are necessarily implied in the original message (Paul K. Jewett, "Concerning the Allegorical Interpretation of Scripture," *WJT*, XV2, 1 (November 1954), p. 13). So *Pilgrim's Progress* (John Bunyan) is a valid allegory: in the Bible's view, the Christian life is a "way," a journey from earth to heaven. But Origen's allegories are invalid, for they set forth a Platonic philosophy in terms drawn from the Old and New Testaments, when biblical teachings are incomparable with the Greek world view in which, for example, the material world is regarded as evil.

Bruce comments that "to Jews this exegesis must have seemed preposterous" (p. 219). He regards it as probable that the Judaizers had applied the Isaac-Ishmael narrative to the Galatians. They would have said "that Isaac was the ancestor of the chosen people; the Ishmaelites are Gentiles. The Jews are the children of the free woman; the Gentiles are children of the slave woman. The Jews have received the liberating knowledge of the law; the Gentiles are in bondage to ignorance and sin. The Jews are the people of the covenant; such blessings as the Gentiles enjoy (like the promise that Ishmael would become a great nation) are uncovenanted mercies ... . The Gentiles of Galatia could not be sons of Abraham by natural descent as Isaac was; yet there was hope for them: they could be adopted into Abraham's family by circumcision and so enjoy the covenant mercies promised to Abraham and his descendants" (pp. 218f.) So Jews would regard Paul's allegory here as invalid. But the validity of his allegory based on the Isaac-Ishmael narrative depends on whether or not Paul's interpretation of this narrative is necessarily implied by its own terms.

4:22–23 For it is written that Abraham had two sons, one by the slave woman and the other by the free woman. ²³ But one, the son by the slave woman, was born by natural descent, while the other, the son by the free woman, was born through the promise.

Paul was surely on firmer ground than Bruce's hypothetical Jewish understanding of the Isaac-Ishmael narrative in regarding the children of Hagar as renegade Jews, rather than as Gentiles. To give all Gentiles a physical linkage to Abraham would prove embarrassing someday for this Jewish interpretation. Paul's purpose in the Isaac-Ishmael story is to emphasize, as in Romans 9:6 ff., that in the Genesis account the children of Abraham, to whom the promises apply, is a group that is at the same time smaller than Abraham's physical descendants (Ishmael and Esau are excluded), and also larger than the physical descendants, for Abraham was to become the "father of a multitude of nations" (Genesis 17:5; cf. 12:3). (The popularly-held Jewish point of view, on the other hand, was stated by Justyn Martyr in his *Dialogue with Trypho* [140]: "Your teachers assert, that those who are Abraham's seed according to the flesh, even if they are sinners, unbelievers, and disobedient to God, will be given the eternal kingdom.") But as the lessened emphasis on the physical linkage in Genesis is honored, then the ethical feature in the true seed of Abraham gains more prominence. Whereas Ishmael was the result of human effort ("according to the flesh" — v. 23), Isaac was born as the result of God's work and faithfulness in fulfilling his promise ("through the promise" — v. 23). So we argue that Paul's message, rather than that of the Judaizers', is a necessary implication of the Isaac-Ishmael narrative.

4:24–26 These things may be treated as an allegory, for these women represent two covenants. One is from Mount Sinai bearing children for slavery; this is Hagar. ²⁵ Now Hagar represents Mount Sinai in Arabia and corresponds to the present Jerusalem, for she is in slavery with her children. ²⁶ But the Jerusalem above is free, and she is our mother.

Here Paul declares that the Jewish establishment, "the present Jerusalem" (v. 25), is not really a part of the promised land, Palestine, but is represented by Hagar and Mt. Sinai in Arabia. In Paul's thinking, the

Jewish establishment, centered in the city of Jerusalem, was under bondage because it felt that its distinctives, such as circumcision and possession of the law, obligated God to regard Jews' sins as forgiven, in contrast to Gentile sins (cf. above, on 2:15). As much as this pleases human pride, the people operating by this system do not have the freedom enjoyed by those trusting in God to live up to the obligation of his promises. After hearing Paul's message the Galatians experienced a superlative blessedness, far above what they are now experiencing as they are about to yield to the overtures of the Judaizers (cf. 4:15). Now they have less joy, because demonic forces, rather than God's power, find the exercise of human pride a compatible atmosphere in which to work (cf. 4:10). (God hates such an atmosphere, because he resists the proud — James 4:6; Psalm 138:6; Proverbs 3:34.) But these demonic forces are weak in comparison with the riches and power which God bestows upon his people (3:5, 14; cp. 4:10).

Furthermore, those who attempt to obligate God's blessing by doing something in which they can boast are loved only by themselves to the extent of the worth of what they produce, but those who trust God's promises are loved by God to the extent of all the joy that God has in extending his blessings to others. Thus those who are the children of the promise are loved as ends, and God rejoices over them to do them good with his whole heart and soul (cf. Jeremiah 32:41). Along this line of thinking, then, Paul regards the present Jewish establishment as in bondage and at far remove from the heart of God, "the Jerusalem that is above" (v. 26), where dwell the children of the promise who are the heirs — Abraham's seed through Isaac. In Paul's thinking only that person is free who is loved fully and for no other reason than the joy God finds in bestowing that love. In comparison to such a person, who is the heir, all others are in servitude, for they never achieve the fulfillment of all joy.

4:27–28 For it is written: "Rejoice, O barren woman who does not bear children; break forth and shout, you who have no birth pains, because the children of the desolate woman are more numerous than those of the woman who has a husband." [28] But you, brothers and sisters, are children of the promise like Isaac.

Here Paul quotes from Isaiah 54:1, where God celebrates the blessed-ness of the once derelict city of Jerusalem, bereft of her children carried off into captivity to Babylon. This Jerusalem, the writing of whose "lesson book" brought to a climax the fullness of time (4:5) after which the peoples of earth could fully profit from the punishments that befell Israel — this is the Jerusalem that shall have far more children (so many from among the "multitude of nations" — Genesis 17:4) than the Jerusalem that seems to be presently prospering. Consequently Paul addresses the Gentile Galatians as a part of this numerous brood of children who are "of the promise, according to Isaac."

> **4:29–30** But just as at that time the one born by natural descent persecuted the one born according to the Spirit, so it is now. ³⁰ But what does the scripture say? "Throw out the slave woman and her son, for the son of the slave woman will not share the inheritance with the son" of the free woman. ³¹ Therefore, brothers and sisters, we are not children of the slave woman but of the free woman.

The present animosity between the Jewish establishment of the actual city of Jerusalem, and the Church comprised of Jews and many more Gentiles, constitutes no argument against her right to be understood as the heavenly Jerusalem celebrated in Isaiah 54:1. At the very beginning Ishmael persecuted Isaac for being the heir. But his persecution did not prevail, for in Genesis 21:10 God commanded the persecuting Ishmael and his mother to be cast out. Paul then encourages the Gentile Galatians to regard themselves as the true heirs of Abraham, even though they are persecuted by the Jewish establishment.

> **5:1** For freedom Christ has set us free. Stand firm, then, and do not be subject again to the yoke of slavery.

The point of the preceding allegory is that only the true sons of Abraham are free in the sense that God fully loves them for no other reason than the joy he finds in extending such love. Only those banking their hope for an eternity of happy tomorrows on God's promises receive such love from God. The rest are not free, for they are enslaved to the need to try to glorify themselves in order to find joy and contentment, without ever succeeding. *"For freedom* Christ has set you free." Here the dative of advantage, or goal, is used, because in the parallel construction of 5:13 the preposition επι with freedom (in the dative) denotes the goal of freedom to which the Christian has been called. "Stand fast, therefore, and do not submit again to a yoke of slavery." The Galatians are commanded to let nothing deprive them of the blessing of being loved by God as an end. They must not become entangled *again* in a yoke of bondage such as weighed them down when they were pagans (cf. Galatians 4:3, 9). They are to remain in this freedom by ever trusting in God and his priceless promises summed up in Christ. But if they submit to circumcision, as the Judaizers are urging them to do, they will take on a distinctive that supposedly calls forth God's praise. This will anger God, who will not give his glory to others (Isaiah 48:11), and it will create in the Galatians an attitude of pride, a context in which the demonic powers feel at home and will thus be able to pare down the Galatians' blessings only to what they deserve for being distinct in themselves — which is a far cry from the blessings that an heir enjoys in the freedom of being loved and blessed by a loving father whose joy is fulfilled simply in seeing the happiness of his children.

Galatians 5:2–6; 5:13–6:18

The passage 5:2–12 comes in between the imperatives of 5:1 and 13, both of which enjoin the Galatians to stand fast in the liberty for which Christ has made them free. Vv. 2–6 set forth theological considerations that make compliance with such an imperative mandatory. Vv. 7–12 argue for remaining in this freedom with several remarks about how deplorable are the Judaizers and their teaching in comparison with Paul.

> **5:2-3** Listen! I, Paul, tell you that if you let yourselves be circumcised, Christ will be of no benefit to you at all! [3] And I testify again to every man who lets himself be circumcised that he is obligated to do the whole law.

The Judaizers were urging the Galatians to be circumcised for reasons that would make it impossible for them ever to have Christ benefit them again. In the way the Judaizers were urging them to be circumcised, there was no thought of how God worked for those who waited for him (Isaiah 64:4), but only of how the Galatians might distinguish themselves the better and thus be more valuable to God. Christ benefits people, however, only as they depend on him to work for them. So the Judaizers were trying to effect a gigantic "role reversal": making God the client, while people become patrons who try to impress God with what makes them distinctive in his sight. When such a reversal is made, it is obvious that Christ is now the worshipper and thus is no longer in the position where he is worshiped for all of his beneficial service to people.

Traditionally Protestants have interpreted verse 2 to mean that if the Galatians felt that to be justified one needed not only to trust Christ but also comply with the demands of the law, then they would be removing themselves from Christ's benefits which come only by faith. This way of interpreting verse 2 appears in the way J. B. Lightfoot went on to interpret verse 3, where Paul says that if the Galatians submit to circumcision, then they become obligated to obey the whole law. He said, "He who willingly ... undergoes circumcision, enters upon a compact to fulfill the law ... . [But] he cannot [now] plead the grace of Christ; for he has entered on another mode of justification" (ad loc.), and instead of experiencing a blessing, he will experience the curse of the law (3:10, ad loc.). Such an interpretation is in line with the reformation view that the law and the gospel both exist in scripture as opposites.

We have often alluded to the difficulties of this view. Betz provides the helpful observation that "it is apparent that in 5:3 [Paul] does not talk of his own view of 'fulfilling the whole law' (5:14), but of a Jewish view diametrically opposed to his own" (p. 260) . The Jewish view is the need to follow up circumcision with an entire acquiescence to the Jewish life-style, which the Jews regarded as supported by the Mosaic law. So the threat couched in "it is necessary to keep the whole law" is the virtual impossibility for any people, like the Galatians, to make a radical change in their cultural profile. One great advantage of this interpretation is that it avoids antinomianism in that it does not put one in the embarrassing position of saying that faith in Christ for justification points one away from the obligation to keep all the universally-applicable commands of the law. Both Paul, the Galatian converts, and the Judaizers were in agreement that the moral, non-Jewish features of the law were obligatory for everyone (cf. 5:14).

So Paul has raised two sobering objections against the Galatians' submitting to circumcision in accordance with the Judaizers' motives: (1) they will remove themselves from the obedience of faith, in which alone they can enjoy Christ's blessings (v. 2); and (2) they all must undertake the exhausting and virtually impossible task of substituting the whole of Jewish culture and customs in place of their own.

> **5:4–6** You who are trying to be declared righteous by the law have been alienated from Christ; you have fallen away from grace! [5] For through the Spirit, by faith, we wait expectantly for the hope of righteousness. [6] For in Christ Jesus neither circumcision nor uncircumcision carries any weight--the only thing that matters is faith working through love.

This really repeats the idea of 5:2 that the frame of mind involved in submitting to circumcision is totally at odds with the frame of mind requisite for being served graciously by God. The moment one tries to receive God's applause by submitting to circumcision, that person then has an attitude that completely rebels against grace. Such a person is thus cut off from God's gracious exertions which bring people to the final enjoyment of perfect righteousness.

5:5 The believer gradually becomes a more righteous person through God's working for that person as he or she lives only by considering the faithfulness of Christ (cf. 2:20, 21). The work of the Spirit already accomplished in us encourages us to look forward to the completion of this work at glorification. Apparently Paul made this statement to counter the Judaizers' claims that the Galatians would have something equivalent to a perfect righteousness the moment they submitted to circumcision. **Verse 6** emphasizes in another way that righteousness is finally effected along the way of faith that has confidence in the love of God and is patient in letting God take time to do his work. Neither circumcision nor uncircumcision have any value in making a person more acceptable to God — in fact, this motive for being circumcised will exclude one from God's grace, since it scorns God's efforts to display his glory which he rejoices in more than anything. But faith working itself out in love indicates that God will eventually make the believer completely righteous. This kind of faith has bright confidence regarding the future because of the way Christ has loved one in the past (2:20).

Negatively, such confidence would eliminate the need to act unlovingly in order to protect oneself (by lying, cheating, stealing, &c.). Positively, such confidence for the future would project itself outwardly in terms of loving actions toward others, because the joy of having such confidence would be doubled by being shared (cf. Acts 20:31). [Note: Calvin was afraid to let love be motivated by faith, because the way Romanism taught people to think in his day, they would then gauge the validity of their faith on how loving they regarded themselves to have been. He therefore allowed faith to affect sanctification only to the extent of giving one the assurance of salvation, so that he or she was then free to let the law goad them on to do loving works. Then the imperfection of one's good works would not cast doubt on a person's assurance of salvation. We affirm Calvin's insistence that faith in God's promises should always give us the assurance of a perfect standing with God. But this faith which brings assurance should also bring about progress in sanctification. Note here that the Greek is saying that faith is working itself out (middle voice) in love. We should see that the imperfection in our works of love stems from our failure to have that full assurance that faith should give us. If Calvin had reasoned along this line, he would then have helped people to maintain assurance by faith and at the same time allowed faith to be the impetus in a person's progress in sanctification.]

(Commentary on vv. 7–11 was reserved for a later writing, but, sadly, never added to this text.)

> **5:12–13** I wish those agitators would go so far as to castrate themselves! ^{13} For you were called to freedom, brothers and sisters. Only do not use your freedom as an opportunity to indulge your flesh, but through love serve one another.

In 5:7–11 Paul has said various things to show the Galatians why they should not heed the Judaizers. He brought his remarks to a conclusion in 5:12 by saying, "I wish that those who would make you *refugees from your inheritance* (the implication of the meaning of αναϛατουντεσ) would also become eunuchs," for then, according to Deuteronomy 23:1, they would be debarred from having fellowship with the people of God. The argument from v. 12 to 13a is that "there is no need for these Judaizers to remove you from your inheritance, *for* Christ has called you to the full enjoyment and freedom of having all that God is as God, which he devotes to your well being (the essence of the inheritance)." Paul strikes this note of freedom again, as he did in 5:1, but the pitfall to avoid here is not legalism but the license of fleshly enjoyments to which people might think such freedom entitled them. So Paul commands in v. 13b not to be deceived into letting the freedom to enjoy the inheritance become a foothold for fulfilling the fleshly desires. Rather, such freedom will be enjoyed fully only as one *serves* others through *the* love.

This love, designated by a definite article, most naturally refers to the love that comes as a product of faith (5:6) (Bruce, p. 240). Genuine love to others is possible only when it stems from genuine faith in Christ. Such love also makes us indebted to seek the welfare of others. This is the sense of the "bondage" under which we should live. We become indentured to others once our hearts have experienced the full joy of possessing the inheritance. Not to share this joy with others by the works of love is as despicable as not repaying a debt, for in both cases we are saying that, in comparison with others, it is *our* welfare that counts more than theirs. Hence Paul declared that he was a debtor to all people (Romans 1:14). But when we graciously extend our joy in the Lord to others through the works of love, then seeing this joy of ours extended increases it even more, so that we do indeed find greater blessedness (and freedom!) from giving rather than from keeping God's joy all to ourselves (cf. Acts 20:35) — just as is true for God.

5:14 For the whole law can be summed up in a single commandment, namely, "You must love your neighbor as yourself."

We should be slaves of others (v. 13c), *for* then we fulfill the whole law (v. 14). A rabbinic tradition a century or so after Paul's heyday cites Leviticus 19:18 as summing up the whole law. It is unlikely, then, that the Judaizers at Galatia would have denied that. the whole law was a necessary implication from the command to love all other people. It would, however, be well-nigh impossible to argue that circumcision was the basis for the whole law, for in Jeremiah 9:26, the prophet shows how circumcised Israel was nevertheless completely disobedient to God. So we see how Paul, on grounds shared in common with Judaism, forbade the Galatian Gentiles to be circumcised, and yet told these same people to fulfill the whole law.

Note. Betz finds it "surprising" that Paul can cite Leviticus 19:18 so easily after all the negative things he has said about the law. "How is the entirely [sic] negative view of the Law, expressed up to 5:12, related to the positive interpretation of the concept in 5:14–6:10?" he asks (p. 274). (We have argued that law was set forth in a positive light in one of the terms of 2:19, in 3:10 and 21, and in 4:21.) So Paul's use of Leviticus 19:18 does not surprise those who have concluded that Paul did use the word "law" in two different senses, often within the same context. See above on 3:21.

5:15 However, if you continually bite and devour one another, beware that you are not consumed by one another.

The second reason the Galatians should serve one another through love is that the alternative is for each person to abuse others, by using them as a means to one's own gratification, and with the result that all but one would be devoured. Bruce admits that this law of love in v. 14 (Leviticus 19:18) "has the same construction as the statutes of the Decalogue and the Torah in general," but he declares that "it is a different kind of law. No external force or sanction can compel the loving of a neighbor as oneself; such love must be generated from within — by the Spirit" (p. 243). Yet verse 15, with its warning that failure to love can destroy all togetherness, is surely an external sanction with the strongest persuasive force. There are several other powerful sanctions in the remainder of Galatians, both positive and negative, for keeping the whole law as summed up in love to one's neighbor.

5:16 But I say, live by the Spirit and you will not carry out the desires of the flesh.

The command to walk by the Spirit is another way to get at the command to love, for 3:2, 5 made it clear that the blessing of the Holy Spirit comes to those who believe; and according to 5:6, true faith will always manifest itself in the works of love. So the command to walk by means of the Spirit implies the command to do the works of love. One fulfills this command as one trusts God's promises (3:5) and makes decisions on the basis of what gives promise of keeping oneself happy in the love that the living Christ will continue to have for one (2:20). The rest of verse 16 is another powerful sanction (or suasive) for thus walking in love, for it declares that such a walk keeps one from fulfilling the lusts of the flesh, which bring misery and shame, and the practice of which, according to 5:19–21, will exclude one from the blessings of the kingdom of God.

5:17 For the flesh has desires that are opposed to the Spirit, and the Spirit has desires that are opposed to the flesh, for these are in opposition to each other, so that you cannot do what you want.

Because of the γαρ introducing it, we understand this verse to be an argument which enforces v. 16's statement that in walking by the Spirit, we will not fulfill the lusts of the flesh. The flesh and the Spirit are unalterably opposed to each other, with the result that "you cannot do the things which you want to do." It seems that this statement is intended to have a double meaning — something that almost never happens in language. When the flesh is in command and lusts against the Spirit, we cannot do the things of the Spirit that we would prefer to do, but when the Spirit is in command over the flesh, then to our delight we find that, despite the great strength of the fleshly lusts, we cannot carry them out. So only through walking by the Spirit will we find the way to overcome the flesh's desires.

5:18 But if you are led by the Spirit, you are not under the law.

The "if" clause here should really be understood as a command, like the first part of 5:16. Concerning 5:16 Bruce said, "One might substitute hypotaxis for parataxis and render, 'If you walk by the Spirit, you will not fulfill the lusts of the flesh'"(p. 243). And with 5:18 so similar to 5:16 one could also say its hypotaxis could be stated paratactically: "Be led by the Spirit, and you will not be under law." We recall that "under law" for Paul meant being under the power of sin (cf. 3:22f.; also 1:4; 4:3, 9), which would mean living demonically, which certainly involves fulfilling all the cravings of the flesh. That 5:18 is indeed a repetition of 5:16 is evident in that in verses 19 through 21 Paul sets forth a catalogue of the "works of the flesh."

5:19-21 Now the works of the flesh are obvious: sexual immorality, impurity, depravity, [20] idolatry, sorcery, hostilities, strife, jealousy, outbursts of anger, self-centeredness, divisiveness, dissensions, [21] envying, drunkenness, carousing, and similar things. I am warning you, as I had warned you before: Those who practice such things will not inherit the kingdom of God! [Fuller]

The following contains gleanings from Bruce's commentary: sexual immorality (πορνεια), all illicit sexual activity; impurity (ακαθαρσια), all vicious conduct that destroys harmonious relations: Bruce cites how perjury was regarded as "uncleanness;" depravity (ασελγεια), vice that throws off all restraint and is unawed by shame or fear: it is not concerned with self respect; idolatry (ειδολολατρεια), which is, among other things, covetousness (Colossians 3:5); sorcery (φαρμακεια), a serious offense in Roman law; hostilities (εχθραι), hostile feelings towards others on racial, political, or religious grounds; strife (ερισ), a spirit that stirs up strife rather than works for peace; jealousy (ζηλοσ), angry resentment that one someone has something one thinks one deserves; θυμοι, outbursts of rage; self-centeredness (εριθεια), promoting oneself by any means possible; divisiveness (διχοςταςιαι), seems to be very close to αιρεςεισ; dissensions (αιρεςεισ) a reproachful spirit to those with different ideas; envy (φθονοι), thinking someone else has what God should have given us, similar to ζηλοσ but without the anger; μεθαι, drunkenness, because it weakens the vigilance needed for moments of moral crisis; κομοι, carousing/revelry.

Paul's list is not exhaustive: there is an indefinite number of similar things which could be mentioned, and so Paul ends the list with "and the like." People whose lives are not controlled by faith and the Holy Spirit, and thus have no power to turn back the desires of the flesh, will have their lives characterized (πραςςοντεσ, present tense, continuous action) by some of these qualities. The words "those that are practicing such things" implies that an occasional and brief slip into one of these works may not be catastrophic. So, generally speaking, one must walk by/be led by the Holy Spirit, or else he or she will not inherit the kingdom of God. Such a consideration provides a powerful sanction for obeying the commands of 5:16 and 18. Another sanction comes from Paul's partial list of the "fruit of the Spirit."

5:22–23 But the fruit of the Spirit is love, joy, peace, patience, kindness, goodness, faithfulness, [23] gentleness, and self-control. Against such things there is no law.

Paul could have called the works of the flesh "the fruits of the flesh" because sowing to the flesh reaps corruption (below, 6:7f.). But since we associate "fruit" with what is pleasing, it was better to speak of the "works" of the flesh, and reserve "fruit" for the results of the Spirit's operation in one's life. The following list comprises some of the attitudes and actions which occur when one walks/is led by the Spirit (5:16–18). Love (Αγαπε) (the general, over-arching term for "love") indicates the affection (cf. 1 Corinthians 13:1–3), and appropriate accompanying action (5:6, 13–14), which occur as one views another person as valuable — not as a means to an end, as the Judaizers were seeing the Galatians; but as ends, as Paul was seeing them. Χαρα (joy) must be a fruit of the Spirit, especially since we walk or are led by the Spirit by exercising faith in the promises of God. In Romans 15:13 Paul talks of how we can have all joy and peace in believing in the God of hope. Patience (μακροθυμια) ("long tempered"). "It embraces steadfastness and staying-power" (Bruce, p. 253). It is the word used for a merciful person who is slow to anger (Proverbs 19:11). Χρηϛτοϛτεσ is "kindness," but it is significant to note that the word comes from the root χραω, "to furnish what is needful." In the lesson book from Israel of Romans 11:17–24, God's "kindness" for those who trust him thus consists in his disposition to work for them and "furnish them with what is needful." "Useful kindness" is what all those who are in Christ can expect for eternity (Ephesians 2:7). Then as God is "kind" toward us, we should show "kindness" toward others by making ourselves truly useful to them from time to time. Goodness (αγαθοϛυνη) is the antithesis of φθονοσ ("envy") and thus stresses the idea of being generous in exercising our usefulness to others. Faithfulness (πιϛτισ) here has the solidly ethical quality of being faithful, or dependable.

5:23 Πραυτησ (meekness/gentleness). Bruce quotes Aristotle as defining this quality to be "the mean between excessive proneness to anger and incapacity to anger." Jesus who was meek and lowly in heart (Matt. 11:29) was perfectly capable of indignation (Mark 3:5). Εγκρατεια ("self control"). It represents what athletes do to ready themselves for physical competition (1 Corinthians 9:25). It has to do with control over the more sensual passions, and is used in 1 Corinthians 7:9 to exhort those who cannot restrain sexual passion to marry. —"*Against which there is no law.*" Bruce says that by this Paul means "that when these qualities are in view we are in a sphere with which law has nothing to do. Law may prescribe certain forms of conduct and prohibit others, but love, joy, peace, and the rest cannot be legally enforced" (p. 255). But we have already seen the sanctions by which love is enforced in the preceding verses, and as for the enforcement of joy, see Deuteronomy 28:47f., "Because you did not serve the Lord your God with joyfulness and gladness of heart by rea-

son of the abundance of all things, therefore you will serve your enemies whom the Lord will send against you ... in the want of all
things." So we argue that Paul's double negative, "against which there
is no law," signifies that the fruit of the Spirit consists of qualities,
each of which is enjoined by the law of faith, which sets forth the profile of the obedience of faith (5:14). (So Betz, ad loc, p. 288.) That the
fruit of the Spirit complies with the law constitutes another sanction
for obeying the commands of 5:14, 16, and 18.

5:24 Now those who belong to Christ have crucified the flesh with
its passions and desires.

Union with Christ (2:19–20; 3:16, 26-29; cf. 4:19–20) brings the
power of Christ into the heart, and only this power is sufficient to
hold back the forces of evil (cf. 1:4; 3:22; 4:9; 5:16, 18). As we have
said before, we experience the reality of this power as we deliberately
trust a promise of God that pertains explicitly to some situation where
we consider resorting to the flesh to receive the resources needed for
coping. We must remember from 3:5 that we receive the abundance
of God's Holy Spirit as we exercise a hearing of faith.

5:25 If we live by the Spirit, let us also behave in accordance with
the Spirit.

Στοιχομεν (rendered "live" here) conveys the idea of marching in step
or of ordering one's life; this is a much more specific imperative than
the English words "live" or "walk" connote. While a certain amount
of time management is wise, we must not be so locked into a schedule
that we are unable to "be instant in season and out of season" (2 Timothy 4:2). Neither our reasoning powers nor the commands of the
scripture can do more than give guidelines for how to conduct our
daily life. We must let the leading of the Holy Spirit show us the precise steps we are to follow as unexpected contingencies arise. Verse
25 comes back to the high-level, imperative status of 5:13, 16a, and
18a.

5:26–6:1 Let us not become conceited, provoking one another, being jealous of one another. Brothers and sisters, if a person is dis-
covered in some transgression, you who are spiritual restore such

a person in a spirit of gentleness. Pay close attention to yourselves, so that you are not put to the test too.

At 5:26 Paul shifts from giving the most all-inclusive ethical commands ("through love serve one another" — 5:14; "walk by the Spirit" — 5:16; "be led by the Spirit" — 5:18; "order your life, step by step, by the spirit" — 5:25) to some specific commands. The first negative-positive set of specific commands is directed against pride in two of its manifestations. Such commands are appropriate at the end of an epistle directed at overcoming Galatianism, the error of rejecting dependence on God and striving instead to show what worth we have toward him. "Do not become conceited." A person never has any justification for feeling proud in oneself, for everything one has, one has received as a gift from outside oneself; therefore people should not glory as though they produced good things by themselves (1 Corinthians 4:7). So all glorying in oneself is empty/vain glorying, but in order to show why there should be no glorying, Paul chooses a term which emphasizes the uselessness of this effort. Paul then states two ways in which this vain-glorying is to be avoided. We should not try to show our supposed superiority by challenging or goading another person to some sort of contest. But envy is also pride, albeit in a reverse way from trying to demonstrate one's superiority. So we should not be envious about some way in which another person seems to have an advantage over us.

We should note that these two manifestations of vain-glorying set people against each other. And so in giving the positive side of this first specific command, Paul enjoins spiritual people to work to restore a believer who has taken some misstep (6:1). It seems that a misstep/transgression (παραπτωμα) would be the first carnal state of one who has ceased to walk by means of the Spirit, so that the flesh now has the ascendancy. This is the point at which a believer should be "repaired," or restored to walking by means of the Spirit.

The implication from the word for "misstep" is that unless it is corrected, it will lead to a stumble, and then a fall. The sooner an "evil heart of unbelief" (Hebrews 3:12) is corrected the better, for when unbelief has sufficiently hardened the heart, some works of the flesh become a practice (cf. 5:21). Servant-love to others (cf. 5:13) must manifest itself chiefly in this readiness to help others to return to a life of walking by means of the Spirit. (Our present-day churches, and especially in this age of the "secular city" [Harvey Cox] in which our friends are no longer confined to the radius of about 500 yards around us [because of the telephone and the automobile], must be urged to organize in small groups, meeting regularly, to do as in Wesley's class meetings, where the spirituality of no more than a dozen people was checked out weekly. Otherwise, loss of joy, which is the first "misstep" of carnality, and may not seem very serious at the outset, will eventually result in outrageous behavior that will call for excommunication unless there is repentance.

But repentance can be very difficult after time has elapsed during which a hardening of heart takes place through the deceitfulness of sin [Hebrews 3:12 f.]). It is a spirit of meekness or lowliness of heart that keeps us in the enjoyment of freedom in Christ (2:5; 5:1, 13), so that we walk by means of the Spirit and are thus "spiritual." All such people are to do "repair work" on the brother or sister who shows signs of having taken the first step in walking by means of the flesh. But as they do this, each must fix attention on him or herself, because it is so very easy to leave our freedom in Christ either by falling into a legalistic frame of mind (5:1) or by fulfilling a desire of the flesh (5:13).

6:2 Carry one another's burdens, and in this way you will fulfill the law of Christ.

By bearing others' burdens in this most loving of all ways (and in other loving ways), we fulfill, the law of Christ, whose basic thesis is Leviticus 19:18, which Paul quoted after commanding the readers to enslave themselves to one another in love (5:13f.). We cannot agree with Bruce that this "law of Christ" has to do with inner motivations and is "not enforceable by legal sanctions" (p. 261). Leviticus 19:18 has to do with inner motivations, and is regarded as necessarily implying the whole law, with all its sanctions. We argue, then, that the "law of Christ" was Paul's designation of the law from this perspective of love for all, rather than from the perspective of the self-conceit of circumcision (cf. 5:3; 2:14).

6:3-5 For if anyone thinks he is something when he is nothing, he deceives himself. ⁴ Let each one examine his own work. Then he can take pride in himself and not compare himself with someone else. ⁵ For each one will carry his own load.

Now comes another argument for obeying Christ's law. The gist of this argument is that the sense of self-worth of each individual is a matter to be considered only in private, before God, and is not to figure in one's relations with other Christians at all. In other words, we must "Bear one another's burdens" in our corporate life as Christians (6:2a), *for* in that corporate life there is no time or energy to be spent in exulting, or in getting others to exult, in one's own worth. Paul commences this argument (6:3) with the warning of how easy it is for people to have a false estimation of themselves. To avoid this (6:4a) it is necessary for each one, privately, to let God show him or her just what he or she really is. Then (4b) that person should rejoice in this God-given appraisal privately, in communion with God, but should never seek for another to join in with one's own rejoicing. For, at the day of judgment, each one will carry his own load; that is, each will have to give an account of himself or herself at God's tribunal.

6:6–10 Now the one who receives instruction in the word must share all good things with the one who teaches it.

As 5:26–6:5 commenced with specific commands (5:26; 6:1) and then generalized them into the "law of Christ" (6:2), so here at 6:6 there is a specific command again: share the fruits of your labors with those who teach you the word. Bruce observes that this is one of the practical things to be done in bearing one another's burdens (6:2). "The teacher relieves the ignorance of his pupil; the pupil should relieve the teacher of concern for his subsistence" (p. 263). Then follows the argument for keeping this specific command of the law of Christ.

6:7–8 Do not be deceived. God will not be made a fool. For a person will reap what he sows, ⁸ because the person who sows to his own flesh will reap corruption from the flesh, but the one who sows to the Spirit will reap eternal life from the Spirit.

We should keep these precepts of the law, for to disobey them is to sow to the flesh and later experience the misery and the eternal punishment that violating them will bring (v. 7). But to obey the commands of the law is to sow to the Spirit and thus lay hold of the blessings of eternal life now and fully in the eternal future (v. 8). The only way, however, that Bruce enlarges on what sowing to the flesh will reap is to allude obliquely to the future judgment of the believer in which negative assessments are to be expected. "Anyone who did not seriously believe in such a coming assessment, or thought that the law of sowing and reaping could safely be ignored, would indeed be treating God with contempt" (p. 265). This is, indeed, part of what mocking God would involve. But the "corruption" of sowing to the flesh must be as antithetical to "eternal life" as the Spirit is to the flesh, and so this corruption must include the real threat of not inheriting the kingdom of God that is directed at all who *practice* the works of the flesh (5:21).

Hence, the better to escape all mockery of God and all self-deception, we must understand that sowing to the flesh results in reaping the eternal punishment that befalls all who do not inherit the kingdom of God. Those who do not take this threat seriously are not banking their hope on Jesus Christ. Paul poses this threat precisely so believers will strive more earnestly to maintain full assurance concerning the hope God has set forth in the Gospel (cf. Hebrews 6:11–12). The Christian will understand that the most effective way not to sow to the flesh is to keep his or her heart fully rejoicing in the Lord and in all that he has promised, including assurance of the forgiveness of sins. Those who reduce such a threat merely to chastisement in the present life, or to loss of rewards at the Christian's future judgment, make it easier for a person to become self-deceived and mock God.

> **6:9–10** So we must not grow weary in doing good, for in due time we will reap, if we do not give up. [10] So then, whenever we have an opportunity, let us do good to all people, and especially to those who belong to the family of faith.

Now comes another general command corresponding to the general command of 6:2; only this command comes after the argument (vv. 7–8) that functions to support both the specific command (v. 6) and the general command (vv. 9a, 10). The Christian must not faint but be steadfast in doing good. Doing good is another way of representing sowing to the Spirit in Paul's thinking, for he speaks of reaping here as in the preceding verse. Bruce agrees that doing good is sowing to the Spirit, but is non-committal on when the reaping shall occur: "Here the eschatological harvest may be in view" (p. 265). We argue that we reap eternal life both by laying hold on its blessings now (cf. 1 Timothy 6:12, 19; and the present tense of "having eternal life" throughout John's Gospel), and by having its fullness in the future. It is unmistakably clear that Paul expects the promise of gaining more enjoyment of eternal life to be the incentive for the patient doing of good works.

> **Note.** The similarity between 6:9–10 and Romans 2:6–10 cannot be ignored. Romans 2:6, "God will render to every man according to his works," is surely like Galatians 6:7–8, where God will see to it that everyone reaps just as he or she sows. Romans 2:7, "To those who by patience in well doing seek for glory and honor and immortality, God will give eternal life," is surely like Galatians 6:9. The misery that the wicked shall experience in Romans 2:8–9 would be an elaboration on the corruption that those who sow to the flesh will reap (Galatians 6:7). Romans 2:10 returns to the theme of v. 7 but this time it speaks of how God will render "glory and honor and peace to everyone who works the good (εργαζο-μενω το αγαθον)," and this is very much like Galatians 6:10, "As we have opportunity, let us do good (εργαζομεθα αγαθον) to all." Romans 2:11, "For there is no partiality with God" echoes Galatians 6:7, "Be not deceived. God is not mocked [for everyone will get just what is deserved and God will play no favorites]." See F. Flueckiger, "Die Werke des Gesetzes bei den Heiden," *Theologische Zeitschrift*, 8(1952), 17–42, esp. p. 37.

In regard to the command to do good "especially to those of the family of faith," should we understand Paul to mean that (1) love terminates its energy as Christians keep doing more good especially to Christians, or that (2) special emphasis is placed on doing good to fellow Christians, to enhance their ability then to reach out to all people? We argue that Paul's implied meaning here is (2), because it fits in better with the theme of Galatians, where the emphasis has been that

God wants to bring his benefits to all peoples. We will accomplish the doing of good to all men more efficiently, in the long run, as we expend a substantial part of our energy and time in benefitting fellow Christians, for then so many more of these will be enabled to do the really loving thing to the peoples of the world in bringing them into the place of enjoying the freedom of having God as one's God. If (1) were true, Paul would then be saying something here that contradicts the desire to get the message out to all the peoples of the world, without playing favorites on account of the distinctives that some have.

Postscript

6:11–13 See what big letters I make as I write to you with my own hand! [12] Those who want to make a good showing in external matters are trying to force you to be circumcised. They do so only to avoid being persecuted for the cross of Christ. [13] For those who are circumcised do not obey the law themselves, but they want you to be circumcised so that they can boast about your flesh.

Betz argues that an amanuensis did the actual writing of Galatians up to this point, but that he followed Paul's precise wording (pp. 312f.). In those days it was sometimes customary at the end of a letter for the author himself to append a paragraph to sum up his case and to make a strong emotional appeal for his cause. Paul writes vv. 12 ff.. in large letters to underscore the importance of what he has to say in these last words (Betz, p. 314).

V. 12 — For Paul the lines drawn between him and the Judaizers are clear. They want to compel Gentile Christians to be circumcised, for this outward, visible distinctive would bring them more praise from their backers in Jerusalem and most of all, supposedly, from God. The alternative for Paul is to withhold ultimate praise from any human criterion for determining worthiness and grant such an honor only to God for being merciful and trustworthy in making and keeping the most benevolent promises toward those who take the undeserving stance of needing mercy. All sinful humanity is carrying out the first alternative in some way. The Christians whose lives run according to the other alternative imply that those living otherwise are enemies of God and all that is truly good. Consequently these enemies persecute Christians, for whom the cross of Christ epitomizes God's merciful grace toward sinful people. In vv. 12–15, Paul's purpose is to draw a sharp contrast between the Judaizers and himself. There is an implied imprecation at the beginning of this Postscript, and verse 12 provides the first justification for it. (The Judaizers are accursed [cf. 1:8], *for* they hate the cross of Christ and care only about looking good in an outward [and therefore irrelevant] way).

V. 13 —Then too, they are accursed because they scorn the law. The ὅι περιτεμνομενοι in the first half of v. 13 is to be understood in the middle voice (not the passive), and they are the same as those who "want you to be circumcised" in the second half of v. 13. So the meaning of v. 13a is "Not even those seeking to have you circumcised are keeping the law," and the way they are violating it comes from the second half of the verse. They are scofflaws in that they are seeking to glory in your flesh by getting you circumcised, whereas the law of faith, the revelatory law, that taught people to glory only in God (Deuteronomy 10:21). (They would also be guilty of "the transgression" about which Paul spoke in 2:18 and elaborated on in 3:8.)

> **6:14** But may I never boast except in the cross of our Lord Jesus Christ, through which the world has been crucified to me, and I to the world.

Paul wants to put himself at a complete antithesis from the Judaizers. God alone will be his praise, for he glories only in the cross, the most concrete symbol of God's gracious mercy. There can be no co-existence between Paul and the world, which lives for the praise of men and not for the praise of God. The cross of Christ has fenced him off from the world, for (1) the carnal nature of Paul, which once loved the things the world holds in high esteem, was conquered by union with Christ in his death (2:19, 20), and (2) his hope for the future rests not on what the world promises but rather upon the promises wrapped up in God's love to him in Christ, who went so far as to be crucified for him. Then too, the world is crucified to him because its love for praise from God (in the wrong way) and people caused it to crucify Christ for paying no ultimate homage to what the world holds in high esteem.

> **6:15** For neither circumcision nor uncircumcision counts for anything; the only thing that matters is a new creation!

This verse gives the reason why Paul wants to regard the world as crucified to him and vice versa. It is that there is nothing in the world, like circumcision or uncircumcision, which has any final value. All that counts is the new creation into which Paul and all who have been baptized into Christ are introduced by virtue of their union with Christ (2:19, 20; 3:28 f.). They experience the new creation through the indwelling Holy Spirit, which is theirs as they respond to God's promises with faith.

> **6:16** And all who will behave in accordance with this rule, peace and mercy be on them, and on the Israel of God.

In 5:25 Paul spoke of how Christians are to walk, step by step, by the Holy Spirit. The Holy Spirit is of the new creation and those who allow him to order their lives will enjoy peace, one aspect of the "fruit" of the Spirit (5:22f.) These are the Israel of God, for they all are of Abraham's seed, in that they all live by faith as Abraham did.

Final Words

6:17–18 From now on let no one cause me trouble, for I bear the marks of Jesus on my body. [18] The grace of our Lord Jesus Christ be with your spirit, brothers and sisters. Amen.

In the command to let no one trouble him, Paul compares himself to the slave of a master who alone has the right to pass judgment on what he does and how he does it. Paul bears in his own body the marks of being the slave of Jesus Christ, the most obvious marks being the scars from his being stoned and beaten (Acts 14:19; 2 Corinthians 11:25). Others who judged him for not concerning himself with the mark of circumcision fail to understand that the marks he bears tie him to Christ and cut him off from the world's concern for things like circumcision. They have no business telling this slave what he should do for his master. This is the sense in which no one should trouble him. Paul's final benediction is that God's grace, conveyed to us through the Holy Spirit, might be a constant source of joy and uplift for our own spirits.

Appendix: Paul's Application of Galatians 3:28

According to Galatians 3:28, "There is neither Jew nor Greek; there is neither slave nor free; there is neither male nor female, for you are all one in Christ Jesus" (RSV). In what sense, we naturally ask, should we understand these negations? Except in the case of "neither slave nor free," they cannot mean erasing distinctions between groups of people.

Help comes in answering this question by realizing that Paul borrowed these three statements from the wording of a baptismal ceremony. There are two other places in the Pauline corpus (1 Corinthians 12:13, Colossians 3:11) where there are such formulaic statements declaring an end to the differences between groups that have been opposed to each other. Baptism is explicitly mentioned in the immediate context of two of these statements (1 Corinthians 12:13, Galatians 3:28) and implicitly in the third.

Concerning Colossians 3:11, Michel Bouttier notes that in its context there is emphasis upon having died, with Christ, to the elemental spirits (2:21–23), and upon having been raised up to heaven, with Christ (3:1–4). Then, because of union with Christ in his death and resurrection, there are exhortations to "put to death" or "put off" the evil practices and affections of the former life (3:5–10), and to "put on" a new set of affections (3:12ff.). In between there comes an argument with language resembling that of Galatians 3:28: "Here there cannot be Greek and Jew, circumcised and uncircumcised, barbarian, Scythian, slave, free man, but Christ is all, and in all" (3:11). Since the writer, both before and after 3:11, is echoing Paul's baptismal language of Romans 6:1–13, Bouttier therefore concludes that "the baptismal formula [of Colossians 3:11] is enshrined in the development of chapter iii." (Bouttier, 1977, p. 8).

Each of the three places where this baptismal formula appears emphasize the idea that every believer enjoys the great benefits which come from being united with Christ, regardless of the person's race, class or gender. So, for example, in Colossians 3:11, believers from races opposite from the Greeks in two directions, the Jew on the one hand, and the Scythian, who is "a particularly uncivilized barbarian" (Windisch,

1964, p. 552), on the other, both enjoy the same blessings of being freed from the elemental spirits. 1 Corinthians 12:13 argues the point of the preceding verse 11 that God apportions various manifestations of the Holy Spirit "to each one individually as he wills," by affirming that "by on Spirit we were all baptized into one body—Jews or Greeks, slaves or free—and all were made to drink of one Spirit." The third statement, Galatians 3:28 comes between two climactic affirmations of the blessings enjoyed by faith in Christ. "In Christ Jesus you are all sons of God, through faith. For as many of you as were baptized into Christ have put on Christ" (v. 27f.). Afterwards comes the affirmation, "If you are Christ's, then you are Abraham's offspring, heirs according to the promise" (v. 29). Therefore the negations of v. 28—neither Jew nor Greek, neither bond nor free, neither male nor female—want to deny that the blessings of being united with Christ depend in any way upon race, class, or gender.

From Cyrsostom to the present, the history of the interpretation of Galatians 3:28 shows a general agreement that each believer, despite his or her distinctives, should rejoice in the all-inclusiveness of God's blessings attained simply by faith in Christ. Divergent opinions emerge, however, in understanding how the neither-nor combinations should affect the attitude and behavior of one believer toward an opposite in the pairs mentioned. Can a slaveholder own a slave who, like him, is a member of Christ's body? If God dispenses his spiritual gifts "to each individual as he wills," then should a church be on the lookout, among the women as well as the men, for those having the gifts requisite for official ministry? In this century there is disagreement in many American churches over this question, as in the 19th century there was disagreement in many American churches over the application of "neither bond nor free."

Since the affirmation of this baptismal formula was so important for Paul that he (or his school) used a form of it three times, we believe that we should go to his writings to learn what we can of how he wanted the negations of Galatians 3:28 to be applied between believers in the matters of race, class, and gender. Like Michel Bouttier (but with different results), "we would like to review quickly how Paul himself received and lived out those few and various passages, pertinent to Galatians 3:28, by which we catch a glimpse of his thinking" (1977, p. 16).

I. "Neither Jew Nor Greek"

Galatians, chapter two, provides specific information on how Paul applied oneness in Christ to relations between Christian Jews and Gentiles. During his visit to Jerusalem, a certain group of Christian Jews (termed "false brethren" [2:4]) sought to have Titus, a baptized Gentile, circumcised. They wanted circumcision, in addition to baptism, to comprise the sign of the covenant. Making each Gentile believer submit to circumcision as well as baptism would have greatly impeded Paul's Gentile mission and, very possibly, stopped it altogether. So Paul resisted all efforts to have Titus circumcised, " that the truth of the Gospel might be preserved for you [Gentiles]" (2:5).

Paul's efforts succeeded, and Christian Jews had to accept the uncircumcised Titus as being fully an heir of the promises to Abraham's seed as any Jew. Paul also required a similarly profound change in a Jew's attitude and behavior toward a Gentile, when the situation arose where a Christian Jew, residing in the Diaspora, belonged to a church comprised of many baptized Gentiles, like that at Antioch (cf. Galatians 2:11–14). Because early Christians ate some meals together in their household churches, Paul, Peter, and other Christian Jews, joined with Christian Gentiles at these meals and ate whatever was served. Christian Jews at Jerusalem, however, were so troubled to hear this that they sent a group to Antioch to inquire about this matter. As a result, Peter stopped eating with the Gentiles, perhaps to avoid the possibility of splitting the Jerusalem church. But Paul understood that Peter, in so acting, was telling the Gentiles that in order to become bona fide Christians, faith in Christ was not enough; they must also assume Jewish cultural distinctives. For Paul this was not being "straightforward about the truth of the Gospel" (Galatians 2:14). It denied the cardinal affirmation that justification and sanctification were by faith alone, thereby placing such impediments in the way of a Gentile's becoming a disciple of Jesus that the Great commission could not be carried out.

Thus Galatians, chapter two, makes it evident that Paul insisted upon a full compliance with the meaning of the affirmation that "in Christ there is neither Jew nor Greek." A refusal to submit to this meaning denied the gospel and destroyed the Gentile mission. So Bouttier, it seems, makes only a start in applying Galatians 3:28 when he says, "The presence, in the congregation, of those by whom one finds himself offended or accused, provides the opportunity for each to express his new freedom [in Christ]; the Jew can do a favor to the Greek, and the Greek, to the Jew [and son for slaves/masters and men/women]" (1977, p. 17). But he seems to stop short of Paul when he says, "Being made one in Christ does not destroy the ties of a Jew with Israel, of a slave with the oppressed, or of a barbarian with the ostracized" (p. 18).

II. "Neither Bond Nor Free"

In his ninety-page treatise on Galatians 3:28 (1978), Hartwig Thyen has no difficulty in finding a coherent Pauline teaching regarding the implications of baptism for slaves and masters. For one thing, since he regards the prison epistles (excluding Philemon) and the pastorals as having an author whose outlook differed sometimes from Paul's, he can ignore the instructions for slaves and masters found in Ephesians, Colossians, and 1 Timothy. He also rejects interpreting 1 Corinthians 7:21b as saying, "But if you[slaves] can gain your freedom, make use of [your present condition of slavery] chapter 7 has a dozen commands for people to remain in the state they were in when converted. But Thyen understands Paul to be giving a parenthetical exception to this rule in v 21b, because he introduces it with a "but" (ἀλλά) followed by a conditional "if" clause. Furthermore, there are six other places in chapter 7 where Paul enjoins people to change their status under certain circumstances. So Thyen would follow the RSV's translation of v 21b: "But if you can gain your freedom, avail yourself of the opportunity."

Philemon provides Thyen with a confirmation of this translation. To Philemon, the slave owner of the runaway Onesimus, who had become a Christian, Paul said, "You ... might have him back forever [if you do not insist on his severe punishment], no longer as a slave but ... as a beloved brother ... both in the flesh and in the Lord" (15f.).

Paul also said that he had confidence that Philemon would do "even more than I say" (21). So Thyen concludes that "a necessary inference from Galatians 3:28 in the context of Pauline theology appears to be that at least among Christians there ought to be nor more slavery" (p. 166).

This abolitionist stance would then be the necessary implication of "neither bond nor free" in Paul's thinking. Indeed, Hans Dieter Betz argues that this negation "when heard by Christtian slaves at the ceremony of their baptism … could hardly be misunderstood" (1979, p. 195). There is no evidence, however, that abolitionism ever got a general hearing in the early churches. Instead, Ephesians, Colossians, 1 Timothy, and 1 Peter have passages which allow the continuation of slavery, though they seek to mitigate its miseries with injunctions based on the future judgment, Christ's example of suffering wrongfully, and the need for a blameless Christian testimony before the world.

Furthermore, Paul Jewett (1975) would disagree with Thyen that the evidence in Philemon and 1 Corinthians is sufficient to show that Paul openly and explicitly advocated abolitionism. Jewett remarks that Paul's "polite reserve" in obliquely suggesting that Philemon manumit Onesimus "contrasts with the direct encounter Paul had with Peter over Jewish/Gentile relationships at Antioch (Galatians 2:11f.)" (p. 139). As for 1 Corinthians 7:21b, Jewett believes that the apostle may well have meant that a slave should take advantage of any opportunity for freedom, but since he does not expand on this at all, "obviously Paul is more interested in one's spiritual status of freedom in Christ than in the social implications of this freedom" (*ibid.*, note).

The evidence, therefore, seems clear that Paul was not concerned with carrying out the baptismal implications of "neither bond nor free." This conclusion would be reinforced to whatever extent the teachings of Ephesians, Colossians, and 1 Timothy regarding slaves and masters echo the apostle's own teachings. But when we consider the third negation in Galatians 3:28, "neither male nor female," we find from 1 Corinthians, an uncontested epistle, that Paul was as disinclined to enforce the implications of this negation, as the contested epistles are to enforce "neither bond nor free."

III. "Neither Male Nor Female"

In 1 Corinthians 11:2–16 Paul teaches that a woman is subordinate to a man, and that in showing this submission she reflects a man's glory, as the man, submitting to Christ, reflects the glory of God. In keeping with this patriarchal submission, 14:33b–35 teaches that women are to keep silence in the church's stated meetings, and are to receive help in understanding Christian teachings from their husbands, at home.

Hartwig Thyen, who is concerned to apply the baptismal implications of Galatians 3:28 fully to the churches, is distressed to find Paul teaching patriarchalism and backing it up with theological arguments in these two passages in 1 Corinthians. He laments how Paul has thus caused his followers "down through the centuries and up to the present to discriminate against women" (1978, p. 180). In these passages Paul argues that since the woman was created *from* the man in Genesis 2, therefore she is subordinate to the man in the very order of creation itself (1 Corinthians 11:8). Thyen notes that this is generally in keeping with the rabbinic idea that women are subordinate to men. For him this means that "[Paul] has given his opinion here 'according to the flesh' … and not according to the Spirit," because "his exegesis, in which only the man is made after the image of God, and is the one to represent the divine glory, is unequivocally opposed by Genesis 1:27, which sets the pattern for construing Genesis 2 by explicitly saying that Man [*Mensch*] as man and woman was created in the image of God" (pp. 184ff.).

Why did he not explore the possibility that Paul was accommodating his teaching, for the time being, to patriarchalism, so as to channel the church's energies toward the crucial task of bringing the attitude and behavior of Christian Jews and Gentiles into harmony with "neither Jew nor Greek"? Accommodation was a foundation of Paul's ethical theory (1 Corinthians 9:19–23; 10:32–11:1), and Galatians and Acts provide examples of how Paul used this principle to maintain the integrity of the gospel, the unity of the church, and the ongoing movement of the Gentile mission. Consequently, before concluding that Paul was teaching "according to the flesh" in enforcing patriarchalism, Thyen should have considered whether or not 1 Corinthians 11:2–16 and 14:33b-35 are not an instance of temporary accommodation to what is less than consistent with the baptismal implication of "neither male nor female."

Like Thyen, Jewett affirms that Paul's teaching about women in 1 Corinthians finds its roots in rabbinism. But unlike Thyen, he sets forth the outline of a theodicy for why it was necessary for God to accommodate himself, temporarily, to the evil of patriarchalism. To begin with, God was incarnated as a man, says Jewett, not because a man is more like God than a woman, but because God had to come into "a history marked by sin and alienation [involving patriarchalism]" (p. 168). Then in regard to the all-male apostolate, Jewett argues that that indeed "our Lord's intent, through the preaching of the apostles, was to redeem mankind and so create a new humanity in which the traditional antagonism of the sexes would be reconciled." But since this redemption could not be accomplished by a "simple confrontation" with patriarchalism, "one can understand, then, why [Jesus] chose only men to herald the truth of the Gospel in the Greco-Roman world of the first century" (p. 169).

The third part of this theodicy is the affirmation that "it is from this perspective [of *God's* temporary accommodation to secondary problems in the sinful world] that we must understand the pronouncements of Peter and Paul, leading apostles, to the intent that women should keep silent in the church and not aspire to the teaching office" (p. 166). After analyzing the various arguments Paul used to support patriarchalism, Jewett says, "All of these considerations are viewed by Paul as indicative of the relationship which *God intended* to prevail between men and women" (p. 51, emphasis added). But from God's point of view such patriarchalism was only temporary; someday the churches would come to understand the full implication that "in Christ there is neither male nor female." So Jewett concludes his book saying, "while Paul went all the way in living out the truth that in Christ there is neither Jew nor Greek, he by no means denied in his life style [of treating individual women as peers] the implications of the further truth that in Christ there is no male and female. ... But [now] it is high time that the church press on to the full implementation of the apostle's vision concerning the equality of the sexes in Christ" (p. 147).

IV. Accommodation Ethics

"Accommodation" is the word best suited in the English language to represent Jewett's understanding of God's strategy in incarnating his only Son as a male, and in appointing an exclusively male apostolate. For Jewett the term "accommodation" would also apply to God's decision to permit Paul and Peter to teach a Christianized version of patriarchalism that was to be valid for a temporary time only. The term represents what people do who have identified themselves with one belief and behavior structure, and "yet ... employ the language of [another structure], or conform to its patterns of thought and behavior at certain points" (Peter Richardson and Paul Gooch, 1978, p. 100).

The philosopher Gooch notes that "in so far as [these two structures] are themselves inconsistent structures, then whoever accommodates [from one to the other] will be considered inconsistent" (*ibid.*) For example, the God who created men and women as equal components of humankind could easily appear inconsistent to have ordained an all-male apostolate. Then too, since accommodation stops short of being a conversion in which one leaves behind one belief and behavior structure and espouses the other, then whoever "accommodates without wholeheartedly changing his beliefs about what he ought to do ... may well be accused of hypocrisy" (p. 111).

So people might well charge God with hypocrisy for creating males and females equally in his image (Genesis 1:27), and then ordaining Paul to command "in all the churches" for women to remain silent in stated meetings because "they are subordinate [to men], even as the law says" (1 Corinthians 14:33ff.). The way Paul's thinking worked in supporting female subordination from the high religious sanction of the law is seen in 1 Corinthians 11:8f. Since, according to Genesis 2:20ff., the woman was made *from* the man and thus *after* him, therefore the "woman [was created] *for* the man."

Gooch observes, however, that "on occasions someone's [accommodating] actions may appear inconsistent [and hypocritical] only because some reconciling principle is not known to the observer" (p. 112). But we know the loving principle on which God acted in accommodating himself temporarily to patriarchalism. There is ample evidence to show why God, in supporting a Christianized version of patriarchalism, enforced by apparently scriptural sanctions, was not being at all hypocritical but was acting out of concern to do the most benevolent thing for the human race in the long run. What needed most to be done in launching the Great Commission, was to show that Gentile believers enjoyed the same status in Christ as Jewish believers simply on the basis of faith alone. Had this point not been made explicitly and emphatically, Christianity might well have remained an obscure Jewish sect for a few decades, and then disappeared. Then the nations of earth would have been deprived of the blessings of Christ. Surely everyone rejoices that God risked the charge of being hypocritical by temporarily accommodating to patriarchalism ad supporting it with plausible, but not persuasive, scriptural arguments. Had he not done this the outworking of redemptive history would have stopped.

So, from the outset, there had to be a direct and protracted confrontation against the Jew/Gentile rift. We have already noted, under "Neither Jew nor Greek," the changes in attitude and behavior that a Jew underwent in order to belong to a church where there were believing Gentiles. Since all this energy had to be expended, for a number of decades, on order to forge out the full implications that "in Christ there is neither Jew nor Greek," it was essential, then, for God temporarily to enforce upon the fledgling churches a Christianized form of patriarchalism (and slavery). That women had prayed and prophesied during public worship at Corinth (1 Corinthians 11:5ff.), hints at how strongly Christian women felt the urgency also to forge out the full implications of "in Christ there is neither male nor female." But God, in his love, could not let this pressure burst forth just yet and divert energy away from the most vital task of maintaining the unity of the Church of Jews and Gentiles.

So he imposed the highest possible sanctions to enforce accommodation to patriarchalism. But since these sanctions were only to enforce, for a time, something less than the ideal, they have only the apparent force of a plausible argument, but not the real force of a persuasive one. That women are subordinate to men, because the woman was created *from* the man and *after* the man, has a certain plausibility, but it lacks persuasive force. Although the man was created *from* the ground (Genesis 2:7), no one argues that he is subordinate to it. Then too, what comes *after* is not necessarily inferior. In 1 Corinthians 15:46, for example, the spiritual which comes after the physical is superior.

Paul Gooch remarks that since biblical accommodation (1 Corinthians 9:19–23; 10:32–11:1) must be undertaken only temporarily in order finally to move people into the full implications of freedom in Christ, it "has to be accompanied by additional procedures ..." (p. 115). Otherwise accommodation will only confirm people in their substandard way of living. In other words, accommodating teaching must be accompanied by clues indicating that this teaching is being tolerated only temporarily until the true teaching can be established. One such clue could well be the shakiness of Paul's exegetical argument from Genesis 2 in support of patriarchalism.

Another clue comes from understanding why (as stated above) Paul went all the way in enforcing "neither Jew nor Greek," but accommodated the handling of slavery and patriarchalism. This is not difficult to suppose, for Paul forthrightly told how he became "as a Jew" to the Jews (1 Corinthians 9:20). He also urged his readers to imitate him as he imitated Christ in becoming "all things to all men, in order that he might save some (1 Corinthians 9:22; 10:33–11:1). When one understands Paul's application of Galatians 3:28 from this standpoint, then two other clues appear which should have signaled to the church down through the centuries that patriarchalism clashes with the freedom of the gospel.

One such clue is seen in Paul's failure to enforce the rule of 1 Corinthians 14:34 by rebuking the women who had prayed and prophesied in public. In 1 Corinthians 11:2–16 he reproved them only for not wearing headgear signifying submission to men. A good explanation for this is that Paul knew perfectly well that God gives his spiritual gifts (including ministry gifts) "to each one, individually, as he wills" (1 Corinthians 12:11). Consequently, he could not rebuke them for what was done in all probability as a work of the Spirit. So he simply rebuked their lack of patriarchal attire, and later on in the book forbids women in general to speak ina meeting. The most loving thing to do at that time was to keep Galatians 3:28 from applying to patriarchalism, so that all the church's energy might be spent in making "neither Jew nor Greek" a reality.

Then there is the clue of Paul's own behavior toward women. Paul greets several women by their own names at the conclusion of Romans (Ch. 16), whereas the rabbis spoke of a woman only as the wife of a certain man. Unlike a rabbi, Paul addressed a group of women with no men present (Acts 16:21), and he accepted Lydia's invitation to be a guest in her house (Acts 16:15). He regarded both Pricilla (Romans 16:3) and Timothy (Romans 16:21) as "my fellow worker." Since both are known as teachers of the word (Acts 18:26; Philippians 2:20), it is natural to understand this as the labor in which they supported Paul.

How, then, did Paul apply Galatians 3:28? We answer that he fully enforced "neither Jew nor Greek." With regard to "neither bond nor free" and "neither male nor female," he supported, by way of accommodation, a Christianized slavery and patriarchalism, but with regard to both he left sufficient clues for the church to have understood that these teachings no longer applied after the "neither Jew nor Greek" issue had been settled.

Bibliography

Betz, Hans D. *A Commentary on Paul's Letter to the Galatians*, Hermeneia. A Critical and Historical Commentary on the Bible. Philadephia: Fortress Press, 1979.

Bruce, F.F. *The Epistle to the Galatians* (The New International Greek Testament Commentary), Wm. B. Eerdmans Publishing Co., 1982.

Bouttier, Michel. "Complexio Oppositorum: sur les formules de I Corinthians XII.13; Galatians III.26–8; Colossians III.10.11." *New Testament Studies*. 23 (1977), 1–19.

Burton, Ernest De Witt. *A Critical and Exegetical Commentary on the Epistle to the Galatians* (The International Critical Commentary), T & T Clark, 1921.

Gooch, Paul. "The Ethics of Accommodation." *Tyndale Bulletin*. 29 (1978), 89–117.

Jewett, Paul K. *Man as Male and Female*. Grand Rapids: Wm. B. Eerdmans Publishing company, 1975.

Richardson, Peter; and Cooch, Paul. "Accommodation Ethics." *Tyndale Bulletin*. 29 (1978), 89–142.

Schlier, Heinrich. *Der Brief an die Galater*, 5th ed. (Kritischexegetischer Kommentar uber das Neue Testament 7), Gottingen: Vandenhoeck and Ruprecht, 1971.

Thyen, Hartwig. "… nicht mehr männlich und weiblich." Eine Studie zu Galater 3,28. *Als Mann und Frau geschaffen*. F. Crüsemann and H. Thyen, eds. Gelnhausen: Verlagsgemeinschaft Burkhardthaus, 1978. Pp. 107–197.

Windisch, Hans. "*barbarous*." *Theological dictionary of the New Testament*. G. Kittel, ed., and G. W. Bromily, ed., and tr. 8 vols. (1964–74). Grand Rapids: Wm. B. Eerdmans Publishing Company, 1964. I, 546–53.

Made in the USA
Lexington, KY
30 June 2016